9.50

MORE THAN
SKIN DEEP

More Than Skin Deep

Kendall McDonald

PELHAM BOOKS

First published in Great Britain by
PELHAM BOOKS LTD
52 Bedford Square
London, W.C.1
1971

7207 0445 6

Set and printed in Great Britain by
Tonbridge Printers Ltd, Peach Hall Works, Tonbridge, Kent
in Baskerville eleven on thirteen point on paper supplied by
P. F. Bingham Ltd, and bound by James Burn
at Esher, Surrey

*Particularly for Penny—but
also for all those others who
have been brave enough to let
me dive with them*

Illustrations

MAPS AND CHARTS

Chapter

One

I can tell you even now the colour of the bottom part of her bikini. It was a bright yellow. Not one of those orangey-yellows, but a real yellow yellow. And I suppose that the top was the same colour. But from where I was lying on the sand you couldn't see much of the top. Her long blonde hair hung down over the tiny strap across her back which held the bra up, and she was swaying down to the sea for a swim.

The scene was the South of France and a small private beach outside the holiday resort of Ste Maxime. This is not far from St Tropez, where if they had yet discovered Brigitte Bardot, the French were keeping it to themselves.

The time was shortly after the war. The travel allowance was so small that it wouldn't keep you in wine on a holiday in the same place nowadays. And the drivers of British cars used to wave to each other on the roads of France because there were so few of us.

I was watching the blonde in the yellow bikini with admiration. But my admiration was silent because her husband, André, was lying on a towel next to me and though I knew the French were civilised about that sort of thing, I was not yet sure how far that civilisation went. I know now, of course, that if I had expressed my admiration of his wife's figure, André would have taken it as a great compliment – especially in view of the fact that his two young sons were involved in some complicated game in the shallow water nearby.

The blonde was Francoise Delille, the Comedie Francaise actress, and here, away from Paris, she followed each morning a restful routine of sunbathe, swim, sunbathe, swim, until it was time for lunch.

The sunbathing minutes were now over and the swimming was about to begin. As she plunged into the water, the spell was broken and my attention wandered to her children.

9

I think that I can honestly say that this was my first sight of a mask and snorkel tube and any form of underwater swimming. I got up and wandered down the beach to see what they were doing. Years later they were to become very expert indeed, but now there seemed an incredible amount of choking and coughing and gasping for air involved in very short cruises on the surface of the clear flat-calm sea.

I asked questions in my schoolboy French and found that schoolboy French is adequate in these circumstances – when speaking to a French schoolboy. My questions did not evoke the usual smiles, which I got from adults and which I liked to pretend to myself were caused by my unusual French accent, but were answered with all the seriousness that a small boy can give to a subject of which he is the master and the adult the sincere pupil.

The question and answer session ended with them handing me the mask and breathing tube and being offered the freedom of that particular stretch of the Mediterranean.

I don't know quite what I expected to see when I struck out from the shore with a funny sort of breast stroke designed to keep the tip of the tube above the water. I had been solemnly warned by the freckle-faced Didier that this was an essential part of the art for a beginner like myself and it would be wiser if I did not actually plunge beneath the surface until I had mastered the surface technique. (He knew what he was doing that lad. The same style of instruction is usually given by experts to beginners today)

I looked down. I could see! I saw sunlight patterning seabed like a golden outlined jigsaw. I saw valleys of sand and mountains covered with green weed like forests. And more – I saw fish!

I saw gaily coloured Mediterranean wrasse that the French call *girelles* and I saw a big green fish, which was another kind of wrasse, but I didn't know it then. And I saw a school of little tiny golden fish all a-twitter of tails around a rock – baby bream, which the English call goldline and the French *saupe*.

It seems silly somehow to say that at that moment in water that was little more than chest deep, and wearing a child's underwater swimming mask, which was far too small for me, my life was changed. But it was. At that moment I was 'hooked' on underwater swimming. The next second in my anxiety to see more I ducked underwater and choked on the column of water that shot down the breathing tube into my mouth and throat. But it did nothing to put me off.

For the rest of that holiday I borrowed the children's equipment whenever I could – and at times when I really shouldn't. I found a shop in Ste Maxime which stocked masks, snorkels and fins, and I nearly bought a set of my own. Only the fact that I would have been unable to afford to eat at all on the drive back to the Channel ports stopped me.

That holiday was soon over. But from then on all I thought of in non-working moments was the next one and the clear waters of the Med. In London I managed to buy a mask. It was primitive by today's standards. I bought too a great big metal breathing tube with rubber mouthpiece, and some incredibly uncomfortable war-surplus frogman's fins, which had been left over from the war and were snapped up for sale by a demobilised R.A.F. officer,* who was starting to make a career for himself in the sporting goods business. I remember those fins were so uncomfortable – it was impossible to adjust the heel strap – that I was forced to put a small sponge in each foot-slot to ease the painful pressure on my toes.

And so I went back to the South of France and that little beach belonging to André and Françoise. I felt a real diver and was rather shattered by the better quality of the underwater swimming equipment that was on sale in the shops all along the French Riviera. Young Didier and his younger brother Eric had now added to their equipment a small, but powerful gun with a trident-headed spear.

Diving down to the seabed was now it seemed no longer enough. I borrowed their little gun and felt all the pride of the hunter when I managed to return to the beach with a tiny wrasse as a trophy of my prowess.

It seems odd now to think how keen I was on spearfishing – or how difficult it seemed to be. For the truth is that in those days in the Mediterranean you didn't have to be very good to shoot a fish – rather the reverse, you had to be lousy not to

* Colin McLeod, who is now a director of Lillywhites, the famous sports equipment firm.

be able to do so. But to a man who was trying to find out about snorkelling and spearfishing the hard way – by trial and error – it did seem incredibly difficult.

Obviously I could not go on borrowing the children's gun for very much longer. They never actively protested to me, but the hurt looks on their faces when their mother insisted that they lend me the gun was enough. So I went and bought my own. Then, in terms of travel allowance, it cost a fortune. I was terribly proud of it. Made by Champion of Nice, it was gun-metal blue, had a powerful spring inside the barrel which was compressed by pushing the barbed spear down until it clicked home behind the sear of the trigger.

What is more it had a reel clamped underneath the barrel which carried at least fifty feet of line attached at the other end to the harpoon. This, I felt, was the true mark of the serious spearfisherman and I indulged in gentle daydreams on the beach when resting between swims, in which huge fish tore line off the reel until I had only just enough left to struggle safely back to the surface.

I didn't know it then, but I never saw a really large fish in all my dives off that little beach at Beauvallon, and it is highly unlikely that I would have done so at the best of times. There was a reef of rock at one end where a magnificent villa rose from the beach like the walls of Dartmoor Prison and there were scattered rocks some way out. But most of the underwater scenery consisted of hillocks covered with the long green thin leaves of eel-grass and the sand-mud floor of the valleys in between. It was not real fish country. Not the sort of Spanish rock-piles that I was to hunt over later and which provided cover for all kinds of big fish.

There were fish there, of course, but they were mostly wrasse and other little ones that took shelter in the eel-grass forests. They provided excellent material for a *bouillbaise*, but not for spearfishing records. The nearest I ever came to a big fish in the South of France was seeing a dentex hurrying along far below me – at a depth I could not have reached even if he had waited for me. But by spearfishermen's standards in those days he was not really a big fish, a mere two-footer.

The nearest I came to bringing home a really worthwhile trophy was when I found – to my astonishment and fear – an ugly large red *rascasse* or scorpion fish on the little reef near the villa at the end of the beach. I recognised the fish at once because I had been ploughing with a devotion that my French master at school would never have recognised through Dr Gilbert Doukan's *La Chasse Sous-Marine* which cost me locally 1,000 francs (old ones of course) – though it is true that the presence of Lola Kristo during my studies of the art of spearfishing according to Doukan, helped considerably. It is not every schoolboy who can turn to an attractive feminine French dictionary whenever required!

From Doukan's book and other stories that I had read it was quite clear to me from the moment I set eyes on my first scorpion fish that they were not to be treated lightly. I was not entirely sure whether the fish would attack or not. As it happened in this case the fish sat still – so still that I thought I had missed him when reeling in my line.

André seized upon the fish the moment I walked ashore with it. I was amazed at his apparent carelessness when handling the fish as all the way back to the beach I had been most concerned to keep any part of the fish from coming into contact with me. I was well and truly in awe of the fearsome sting that one could get from the spines on the dorsal fin. But André obviously did not regard it so much as a fish but an essential ingredient of his fish soup. And it is true that a *bouillbaise* without *rascasse* is no real *bouillbaise* at all – according to any expert cook in Provence.

When preparing the ugly fish for cooking – and the *rascasse* is truly ugly for it looks fearsome and scrofulous at the same time (No wonder the scientific name for the fish is *Scorpaena scrofa*.) – the chef must take care to remove the spines and the poison sacs which lie on the back under the dorsal fin.

We dined that night on *bouillbaise* and André had obviously done his work well. It was delicious and none of us crumpled up with stomach pains. I remember thinking what a strange race the French are. Here was a French banker with villa and private beach in the South of France, who obviously found true happiness in the kitchen preparing a fish soup!

Looking back I was, though I certainly didn't recognise it as such, undergoing a course in the art of civilisation. André and Françoise were my tutors in the skills of being happy with primitive things in the midst of luxury, in particular of wines and food. And where they left off Lola Kristo was busy teaching me of the subtleties of French behaviour and the joys of the little bistros and nightclubs in St Tropez itself, introducing me to people like Felix who ran L'Esquinarde in Ste Maxime and now lords it over L'Escale in St Tropez.

And on top of all this I was teaching myself the arts of underwater swimming. Learning to 'shut my throat' when I slid underwater in a duck-dive from the surface so that the water pouring down the breathing tube did not make me choke and gag. Pressing on down until my ears hurt and I could clear then by squeezing my nose and blowing against it as one does in a deep Tube or unpressurised aircraft.

All this crammed into ten days' holiday. No wonder I was tired. And I was beginning to realise one thing more than any other – that underwater swimming, even if it were only snorkelling without the compressed air equipment that was to come later, was so tiring physically that one could not – unless a superman – combine it with late nights in romantic rendezvous.

But I was only beginning to realise this and the excitement of fresh sounds, fresh ideas, fresh ways of living, for a while fought bodily fatigue successfully. After three-and-a-half years of brutalised living in the Army, the French way of life was something to be seized eagerly in the morning and not abandoned until the night-clubs closed.

I had two companions on these early trips into France. First, Frank Owens, now a big wheel in the insurance world. Then, Jimmy Smart, now a highly successful stock-broker, who was perhaps, more than I aware of, grateful for this opportunity to enter into civilisation.

And in case you should think that to my mind then civilisation consisted of night-clubs and bongos, I must set it on record that the meals we ate in the little restaurant that had been created out of the defunct station at Ste Maxime – where grilled meat, haricot verts, and a litre of vin rose were the order of the day – were just as much a part of civilisation as any night-club. Let's be honest. The amount of money we had available didn't stretch to many more exotic meals and if they had I don't know that we would have swapped those meals on a rickety

table in the sunlight under a canopy of dried canes for anything else.

We stayed at the cheapest places we could find. At the little
apartments of Madame Susini just behind the petrol station
near the bridge at the entrance to Ste Maxime or in the smallest
rooms at the Hotel Eucalyptus, further back and up a massive
flight of stone steps. Provence then, as it does now, cooked in
the baking sun and the beach was the order of the day and
replacement of liquid lost in sweat was the order of the night.

It was at the Hotel Eucalyptus that I met a real spearfisherman for the first time. Madame Bethoux who ran the hotel
noticed my mask and flippers and asked if I had met her son,
who was also very keen on hunting fish.

And so I met Raymond Bethoux. A blonde young giant, who
I found out later was the spearfishing champion of the area. I
felt instinctively that he was out of my class, but eagerly accepted
an invitation to go on a spearfishing trip with him. At the
least I would learn from an expert. It turned out, however to
be much more than I had bargained for.

We left the hotel early by my standards – 8 a.m. The reason
for the early start if I understood Raymond correctly was because he had to help his mother later in the day with the affairs
of the hotel (a typically French choice of words and one which
in immediate translation I misunderstood!)

The fact that this was to be a short spearfishing trip starting
from the shore boosted my confidence. It was hardly likely
to involve deep diving if we were just going for a swim from
the beach. For though I could by now clear my ears by pressing
the rim of the mask hard against my nose with one hand –
the gun was in the other – and blowing hard against the pressure
of the mask rubber, this usually took up so much of the air in
my lungs that I was forced to surface shortly afterwards.

We followed the road along the front of Ste Maxime,
past the harbour and on towards Cap Sardinaux. Long before
we got there we stopped and off-loaded all our gear from the
old Peugeot 403B I had bought in London onto a short stone
jetty that looked very old and unused. I say all our gear. Mine
was very simple. My gun, harpoon, mask and fins and metal
snorkel tube (we always called them breathing tubes then)
made up the main items. The only additions were a thin leather

belt from which hung a cork-handled knife and a twisted piece of wire which was to serve as a fish ring and carry my vast catch back to shore.

Bethoux's equipment was much more impressive. To start with his gun was so big that it made mine look like a toy. Without the spear in it came right up to his shoulder. His fins looked more professional, battered and scarred.

I picked one up to have a look. Two or three cuts ran across the upper surface of the rubber just as though someone had been at work with a razor. I looked enquiringly at Bethoux, pointing to the cuts. 'Une grande pastenague,' he said and shrugged as though it was of little importance.

I began to feel less confident. *Pastenague* I could translate easily into sting ray and if the whip-like tail had caused that sort of damage it looked as though Bethoux was an expert in the sort of in-fighting that I would gladly do without.

Another item of his equipment puzzled me. In the place that I would have expected to see a knife on his belt there was a sheath all right, but it was occupied by what I can only describe as a monstrous pair of cutting-out shears or huge scissors. The purpose of these baffled me and I was just about to ask when I realised that unless I hurried I was going to be alone on the stony beach. Bethoux was already adjusting the last of his gear and taking gigantic strides along the jetty towards the flat calm water. At that time in the morning – although one could hardly describe it as the crack of dawn – the Mediterranean did not look exactly inviting. In fact it looked rather cold.

Once in it wasn't bad and I set off in the wake, and I do mean wake, of Bethoux's fins. For a while the fins flailed away just in front of me and I found that I was having to expend a great deal of energy just to keep up. When I lifted my face from the water I could see that we were heading out to sea in the general direction of the Cap itself. Surely he didn't intend to swim all the way there?

But he ploughed on without the slightest slackening of speed and I found myself falling further and further behind. Rather than try and keep up that killing pace I allowed myself to find my own comfortable speed and followed Bethoux by the simple method of taking a surface sight on him every now and then to make sure that we were both going in the same direction.

The seabed was sandy-mud and particularly uninteresting. Common-sense told me that we must be heading for somewhere special – only a maniac would swim all the way to Cap Sardinaux from the point from which we had set out. And he certainly wouldn't do so if he had to get back to help his mother with the chores of the hotel.

Finally Raymond stopped swimming and I began to come within reasonable distance of him. I saw he was waiting for me and spurted the last bit.

This left me so out of breath that I could do nothing but nod with what I hoped looked like enthusiasm as he jerked his thumb downward in a let-fishing-commence gesture. The next moment his fins pointed to the sky and he slid under with scarcely a ripple. There was no doubt that I was watching an expert at work.

I raised my head for a moment to look round and almost panicked when I saw how far from the shore we had come. Cars on the main road from Ste Maxime to St Raphael looked like tiny Dinky toys and the beach was nothing but a distant line. The fact that Raymond was not on the surface left me with a distinct feeling of being all alone in a vastness of sea. In fact my loneliness made me look down quickly for him. The sea was clear, but the seabed was much deeper than it had been before. It looked beyond my diving range, but instead of being flat sand it was now broken here and there by low clumps of black rock. I looked round frantically for Raymond and finally spotted his legs, fins and trunk poking out from under one of the rocks.

As I watched his gun arm jerked and he emerged slowly with a fluttering fish on the end of his long harpoon. It was transferred to his fish ring during a slow drifting ascent.

This lazy rise to the surface marked out immediately the difference in skills between us. If I had been able to stay down as long as he had done – which I doubted – then my ascent would have been a mad race to the surface for air. I obviously had a lot to learn.

I watched him dive three times and each dive produced a fish from seemingly barren rocks. They were corbs. Not big, but obviously large enough for a meal. I was just about to try to get down to at least the top of the rocks when he surfaced quickly, kicking hard, quite unlike his other ascents. On the surface he spat out his breathing tube and shouted over the still surface to me.

'Un poisson tres dangereux!' and he made motions for me to stay away. I almost died of a heart attack as I realised what he had said. A very dangerous fish! A shark?! I wanted to ask him what kind of fish merited that description, but as I finned away from him he was already slipping under the surface again.

This time he didn't go right under a rock shelf, but shot from outside. The end of the harpoon went mad, shivering and shaking all over the place, and when he hauled on the cord attached to the gun, out from the rocks came what looked like eight feet of furious snake.

I knew what it was at once from the French spearfishing books I had read. A moray eel! And a big one!

The trident head of Raymond's harpoon had transfixed it just behind the head in the widest part, but there was no suggestion that the fish had been subdued. If it was possible for it to do so underwater, it was spitting with fury. Bethoux hauled it carefully up towards the surface and just as carefully grasped the end of the harpoon. Then, though he did it all the time, he pulled the big shears from his belt and cut off its head.

I watched in horror as the head fluttered down through the water, mouth still gnashing with venom, until it hit the seabed and lay still. Almost unconcerned, Raymond grinned at me and hung the long body of the moray on his fish ring and then dived down again in search of more fish with the black body of the decapitated moray floating from his belt just as though he had suddenly grown a long tail.

It was at that moment that the spearfishing trip finished for me. I had had enough. I struggled down to the depth of the rocks once and missed an obvious shot that Raymond pointed out to me. As I rose like a rocket to the surface in search of air, he calmly stayed down and nailed the fish I had missed.

Soon after this, he too had had enough. His fish ring was full. On the long, exhausting swim back to the beach I was very conscious of the terrors that spearfishing would now hold. Supposing I came face to face with a moray ... I had no doubt what I would do. And I could only hope that the fish, which had a reputation for being incredibly vicious, would leave me alone to beat a hasty retreat.

Once back at the jetty my legs would hardly hold me up. They felt, as people say, like rubber. You would think, however, that Raymond Bethoux had been for a little swim in a pool for all the difference that the long swim had made to him.

On the way back to the hotel – I felt more like a sleep than coffee and croissants for breakfast – Raymond told me about morays. I tried to catch every word, but my French was not up to some of it. I gathered that he considered moray eels liable to attack without provocation and added that a friend of his had once disturbed a number that were breeding and the whole pack had attacked him. He was in hospital for some time. Having seen the moray's head in action, I could well believe it.

What Bethoux said only confirmed what I had read then about this fish, but later experiences tell a different story.

Morays can be black, brown or mottled with yellow streaking or blobs. They inhabit any depth, are usually only found in Mediterranean or tropical waters and can indeed be found in very shallow water. They are not normally aggressive, but certainly look it. They are generally found in dark holes or caves with only their head sticking out of their chosen territory.

Morays have a habit of opening and closing their mouth which displays their teeth, but it appears to be nothing more than a natural movement. Some observers have suggested that opening and shutting of the mouth is a method of forcing more water through their gills and so preparing their body for action.

Though most spearfishermen at the time when I first dived with Bethoux believed that the moray carried poison fangs among its teeth – some very positive statements asserted that there were two fangs in the roof of the mouth like the fangs of some snakes – there is no truth in the story at all.

Scientists believe that if bites do indeed go septic after a moray bite this is more likely to be because of decaying food particles on the teeth rather than any toxic mechanism.

Opinion is now changing, too, about the aggressive nature of the moray. Most bites seem to occur because a hunter or aqualung diver puts his hand, literally, on to a moray in the darkness of a cave rather than because the moray attacks on sight.

Even more recently diving scientists have found that some

morays will allow themselves to be stroked 'behind the ears' and positively 'purr' with pleasure at this tickling. I would suggest however that this kind of experiment is not carried out by the average diver or spearfisherman. The one you pick to try it out on may be the non-stroking kind!

However, at the time I knew none of this – and neither did Mediterranean spearfishermen that I met. I was most impressed by the obvious fury of the moray that Bethoux speared and resolved to have nothing to do with them. The only thing that I could see in the moray's favour was the flavour of that particular one when Raymond's mother served it to me that night. Fried with a squeeze of lemon it was really delicious.

This set-back to my spearfishing career did not last long. After expanding the story into a deadly underwater struggle over drinks with André, Françoise and Lola later that night, I had recovered my nerve enough to be back in the water next morning. But now I realised that if I was going to compete on equal terms with someone like Bethoux I would have to take the sport a great deal more seriously.

So I practised and practised during the rest of that holiday – but improved very little. I don't think I was really cut out to be a champion spearfisherman, but I would never have admitted that even to myself.

Back home the moray story grew and grew and in the end I was not entirely sure that I did not play a heroic part in the struggle myself.

I was now working on the gossip column of the London *Evening News* and found any number of evening 'jobs' that required my attendance. Well if they really weren't all necessary, at least the publicity men of those days were lavish with their invitations to parties – and as a bachelor I really had nothing else to do in the evenings!

It was at one of these parties to launch some improbable starlet, or film, or soap, or new night-club entertainer, that I found myself telling a man about the fascinating underwater world. I can't remember who he was, but I know that he said there was a man in London that I must meet. He was another ... he almost said 'nut' ... This man too was keen on underwater swimming, and he gave me the phone number of a man called Oscar Gugen.

Chapter
Two

Oscar Gugen was of average height, his fairish hair was thinning over a high forehead and he had, I remember, a small neat moustache. He was not exactly the kind of man I expected to meet.

Yet I'm not entirely sure what sort of man I did expect. A huge, tanned spearfisherman perhaps? I don't know. But Oscar Gugen was without doubt an underwater swimming enthusiast. His eyes twinkled and he had a ready grin which went with a slightly sarcastic sense of humour.

The setting for our meeting was in some ways a strange one. It was the early summer and we sat in the garden of the Boileau Arms, Barnes, drank half-pints of beer, and talked spearfishing. At least Oscar did most of the talking and I listened.

He knew far more about spearfishing than I did and had been in there with the real beginners when the only masks were waterproofed welders' goggles and the spearfishermen used home-made handspears. But he talked about all this in a rather off-hand way as though all that was over – as though spearfishing was over in fact – and that the new thing was the aqualung, which was just now starting to come into this country. He was worried about a recent disposal of war-surplus oxygen sets for he feared that few people would realise that oxygen under a pressure of more than 30 feet of water could kill.

(This is believed to be the cause of the death of Commander Jimmy Hodges when filming on an expedition with Hans Hass)

Commandant Jacques-Yves Cousteau who had invented the aqualung in 1943 with Emile Gagnan was a friend of Oscar's and there in the garden of that Hammersmith pub Oscar's eyes lit up as he described the pleasure of using such apparatus. He had already tried out some of the first aqualungs to reach this country in the Finchley Road Swimming Pool and was anxious to form a British club to cope with the flood of people that 'he knew' would want to use it.

Once on the subject of forming a club Oscar was in full spate. He foresaw the need for uniform methods of instruction and wanted to get the club underway at once. As a journalist he thought I could help. Would I?

I would and I left the Boileau Arms full of enthusiasm. Oscar Gugen had made it seem that the whole thing would take flight in a moment and I didn't want to be left out.

I remember writing a story for the News gossip column about this undersea enthusiast and channelled the letters of enquiry that followed to Oscar. But then I had my own undersea adventures to think of – a new holiday was looming up and I was certain that this time I was going to shoot myself a really big fish. So Oscar and I agreed to contact one another on my return and we left it like that.

I went back to the South of France and plunged into a whirl of spearfishing and night-clubs and Lola. It was all very tiring, but highly enjoyable. By the end of the holiday Frank and I were right out of money and slept the last night in the car outside Le Touquet Airport while waiting for a Bristol Freighter to airlift us back to Britain.

Apart from the normal discomfort of sleeping in a car, I had a very disturbed night. I seemed to have some sort of pain in the right side of my chest – rather like a permanent stitch. It was, I told myself, nothing that a little rest wouldn't sort out.

I was now working as a reporter in the News Room of *The Evening News* and day by day the pain got worse until I finally gave way to it and lay in bed with sweat pouring off me. I had no desire to eat, but my consumption of cigarettes soared even higher.

The local doctor came, took one look at me and ordered me to hospital. In Dulwich Hospital I felt so bad that I was only vaguely disturbed by the fact that the nurses who attended to me wore masks each time they came near my bed. I felt so ill that all I wanted to do was sleep and each time I awoke I was, I found, lying in a pool of sweat. My pyjamas were changed every two or three hours, but still I went on sweating.

The pain in the right side of my chest got worse and now it hurt with every breath I took.

I thought in sensible moments that I must be pretty ill and it gradually dawned on me that I was probably an advanced case of T.B.

Doctors inspected me at intervals, thermometers were shoved in my mouth, but all I wanted to do was to sleep. I remember someone saying something about 'streptomycin' and getting a hypodermic syringe stuck into my bottom, but little else.

The next day though was miraculously different. I awoke feeling marvellous, really noticed the nurses – they *were* pretty – for the first time, and wanted to get out of bed. The doctors were pleased, muttered things about 'a fantastic reaction to strep' and decided that I had a pleural effusion of the right lung – fluid builds up between the inner and outer covering of the lung and makes breathing painful – and that the fluid in there must be drained out.

This minor operation, that's what they called it, involved sticking a needle through my back to drain away the fluid. Though once I had been tapped off twice in this way I felt even better.

What had caused the pleural effusion? No one was prepared to say for sure. It could have been a T.B. germ, but after tests they were able to say without any shadow of doubt that I did not have the disease.

During the long months of treatment and convalescence (at St Mary's, Sidcup) which followed I had plenty of time to wonder if I would ever go diving again. Doctors questioned me at length about my history prior to the effusion and seemed particularly interested in the deep suntan which I still bore on my back from the hours of spearfishing in the summer. Excessive sun-bathing they said might have created the ideal conditions for a germ to strike – at least that was the layman's explanation they gave me for a lot of long-sounding medical terms. But finally I was released from hospital with strict instructions not to exert myself unduly for some time to come.

Gradually I came back to full health. But my contact with Oscar Gugen was lost. My next holiday was spent in France but I spearfished gingerly in the shallows and kept out of the sun as much as possible.

In the meantime, though of course I didn't know it at the time, Oscar Gugen had met another journalist, Peter Small of the *News Chronicle*.

(Though I have tried to keep strict chronological order in this book it is important to digress here so that the background can be fully understood.)

With Oscar Gugen as the driving force and Peter Small as the organiser, Oscar's original dream of a British underwater enthusiasts' club became a reality.

Oscar booked a room at the Waldorf Hotel in Aldwych, London, for October 15, 1953 and all known undersea enthusiasts were circulated with the date, place and time of the meeting. About 40 people turned up. I was not among them, but from the records of that first meeting Oscar was obviously at it again.

He stressed the dangers of the new sport of aqualung diving – if enthusiasm was not channelled and directed wisely. His enthusiasm ran away with him as he forecast, prophetically as it turned out, the benefits that could come to mankind from the oceans. He proposed the formation of a club to be called 'The British Sub-Aqua Club'. And his motion was carried.

At a subsequent meeting the rules were accepted and Peter Small was elected Secretary. Oscar Gugen was made Chairman. From these beginnings the British Sub-Aqua Club grew until today it has over 400 branches all over the world, including some in the U.S.A.

Under the later chairmanship of George Brookes, Colin McLeod, Harry Gould and Alexander Flinder, it has trained over 60,000 people in the correct safe use of aqualung equipment, has a current active membership of 15,000 and has been associated with all the great names in the diving field.

The Duke of Edinburgh was its President for three years and is now an honorary life member as is Lord Mountbatten of Burma. Another life member is Commandant Cousteau who has given a great deal of time to the Club. And the Royal Navy has been closely associated with the Club for many years. It is an honoured and honorable organisation.

I was one of the first to join and Peter Small became a friend. But I was not part of the Club in the sense of being one of the organising committee. I did anything I was asked to do to help spread the word, but somehow the aqualung did not attract me all that much.

Why this was so I cannot say. I tried it out in a swimming bath in Chelsea and found the ability to breathe underwater a marvellous thing. But in some way I did not connect the feeling of swimming over the tiles of a London swimming bath with the freedom that I now know only too well that equip-

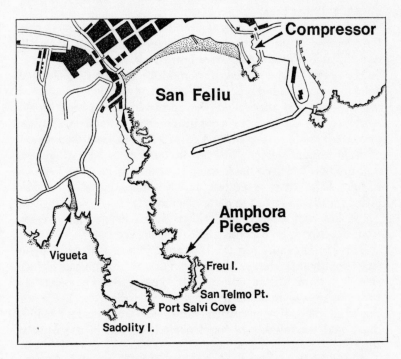

MAP 1. The immediate surroundings of the harbour of San Feliu de Guixols, showing the place where there is a deposit of ancient pottery, the bay where the 'Roman' millstone was found, and the cove where I nearly died of fright.

ment gives to those who want to explore the open sea. A friend, John Messent, was with me on that first personal test of compressed air breathing apparatus and it didn't appeal to him all that much either.

Both John and I returned to our spearfishing not realising what we were missing. I know that I was interested enough to make enquiries from the chest clinic doctor to whom I went for regular check-ups about the possible effect of compressed air on my damaged lung. But though he told me that it was unlikely to harm me and could do some good if used with great care – helping the lung to expand fully and preventing the inhibiting effects of the chalky deposits left in the pleura from the fluid that had collected there during my illness – I wasn't all that keen.

Looking back on it now I know I could have experienced the pleasure of using an aqualung years earlier than I actually did, but it is no use crying over unused air.

My progress in returning to normal life had now accelerated. John Messent had discovered Spain. Only intrepid tourists it seemed ventured there and the spearfishing was out of this world – so he said. There were groupers in a few feet of water and a fish under every rock. And so the next time they went – with John and Doreen Messent on their motorbike, there was I in my new little Austin A.30 right behind them.

John had not exaggerated. It was all there just as he said – there really was a fish under every rock.

He had not exaggerated either the welcome that we got from the friends he had made the previous year.

The Murla family ran the best hotel in San Feliu de Guixols (still do, though they now have built the magnificent Murla Park). Ramon Murla was a curly dark-haired somewhat shy fellow who had married an English girl called Pearl. He was the front man, if you can call anyone so genuine and helpful that – and was always at hand behind the bar in the front of the hotel at the head of the Ramblas.

Josef was the genius behind the scenes. His province was the kitchen. And genius was the word for his cooking. He was married to Selta – one of those elegant women who deserve the Spanish approval of womanhood summed up in their word *guapa*. When Spanish women are elegant they have no mistress in the world.

We were fortunate indeed to meet the Murlas as the first of our contacts in a world which at that time was far behind most of Europe in its standards of living. Ramon would

26

patiently explain to us the ways of Spain, and Pearl would always be on hand to put a lively, if salty, interpretation on what he said. But one of the joys of staying at the Murla was that all the family spoke English and we really had no need of interpreters.

The other contact that John had made on his first visit to San Feliu de Guixols the previous year was Francisco Castello, a broad-shouldered man who owned an engineering firm in the town. Francisco combined all the qualities that made the Catalans different from other Spaniards. He was hard-working, determined, loyal and the farthest thing from the image of the 'mañana' Spaniard it is possible to imagine. And Francisco was potty about spearfishing.

Spearfishing was the major part of those early Spanish holidays. The ritual was always the same. We would talk with Francisco during the week making plans for the week-end, but our daily spearfishing would start with a climb down the hundred steps to the bay of Vigueta.

In those days the climb was hazardous – or we thought it was. Far below the blue Med would shimmer in the morning heat and the steps were so big that they would rush you down at a pace faster than safety set.

Down through the pine trees we would go and always take especial care at the point where, so we had been told, a Spanish boy had fallen down a rain-made gully to crash on the stones of the tiny beach. I know I always used to hesitate at this spot where the rough steps turned right hugging the cliff face. My imagination would picture the scene below where the boy, injured by his long fall, would lie waiting for the boat to come into the cove and take him back by sea to San Feliu and hospital. And I would shiver in the morning sunlight at the imagined scene.

John Messent would usually precede me down – and his wife Doreen, a striking natural blonde in the dark haired world of Spain, would follow carrying packed lunches that the Hotel Murla had provided.

At the end of the steps a large flat rock near the water's edge would be our rendezvous point and Doreen would try to find somewhere to keep the lunches out of the sun and away from the ants that came from nowhere at the sniff of an omelette sandwich. Even hanging the lunch bags on a tree branch was no security – a trail of ants was quite likely to be swarming along the branch and down into the carrier bags when it came to the time to eat.

But all John and I cared about was the spearfishing. Perhaps that is not entirely true. Night excesses had to be paid for in the water during the day.

While John kept to a fairly strict regime of early to bed and early to rise, I found the temptations of 'just another night-cap' difficult to resist – especially when they came from some feminine equivalent of Mata Hari, who, when back in England, turned into a most respectable divorcee. I proved to my own satisfaction that it is possible to fall asleep snorkelling on the surface and paid for the knowledge with a badly burnt leg that took the devil of a lot of explaining to Lola in a year when I was meant to have just popped into Spain to drop some friends before tearing back to the open arms of France!

Late nights, drink, heavy meals, and sexual activity just do not mix with heat, spearfishing and the exertion that goes with it. There's an old Spanish saying that 'Snails and women are no good in hot weather.' The snails they are referring to are the kind that the Catalans are fond of eating in a wine and garlic sauce, but the saying makes its point. The spearfishing was good. And the handing over of loaded fish rings to Josef and Ramon Murla when we finally returned in the early evening was always an occasion for a drink to celebrate a day in the water well spent.

Joseph would cook whatever was possible to cook and our table was always having extra dishes that never appeared on the tourist menu. But times were already changing even in the kitchen. Ramon and Josef Murla tried hard to interest the British tourists, who were beginning to make up the major part of his trade, in the traditional dishes of Spain. But it was a losing battle. 'I am tired,' said Josef to me one night, 'of filling my dustbins with the food they don't want.' And so *paella* and superb dishes like *calamares romanos* (fried squid rings in batter) were slowly disappearing from the pension menus – and from the menus of all the other hotels along the Costa Brava – and cold meats, salads and stews began to take their place.

Among the chefs of the Costa Brava it is widely believed that an Englishwoman died from a heart attack after being told that what she had just eaten with such enjoyment was octopus. And they say that another Englishwoman was taken to hospital after eating a meal of fish. The trouble in this case was that the fish was listed on the menu as *Rape*. The woman enjoyed it immensely – perhaps the name was evocative – and went out of her way to compliment the chef. He, overwhelmed, took her to see the whole fish in her kitchen. She fainted at the sight. The trouble is, of course, that *rape* is the Spanish word for angler fish – and the head with its fishing lure is a revolting sight however delicious the flesh.

It is a sad commentary on modern tourism that even the finest hotels have put most of the traditional Spanish dishes on to the *à la carte* menu and that now the adventurous tourist has to pay extra for the very dishes that were standard fare on the menus put before his predecessors. Perhaps it is poetic justice and a true valuation of real Spanish food compared with the incredible sauce-ridden slop that passes for *haute cuisine* in many places in tourist Spain today.

The early package tour tourists have a lot to answer for – they made the Spaniards lose confidence in their own excellent dishes and surrender completely to 'international cuisine'. The truth is that they could have challenged France by sticking to their own traditional dishes, but now, unhappy as I am to say so, the only way you can get a fine traditional meal in Spain is to go completely *á la carte* or to have Spanish friends who will take you to the restaurants they know which are well off the tourist track.

It is more amusing to note that, almost without exception, the hundreds of thousands of picture postcards that pour back to Britain from Spain's Costa Brava each summer show a flat blue sea. A sea so calm that even where rocks and sea meet no line of disturbed white water can be seen.

I don't suppose it has often struck the holidaymaker who sees waves crashing on those same rugged cliffs during his stay that the picture postcard photographer seems remarkably fortunate in having such perfect weather each time he points his camera at the local scene.

Of course it is all part of the projection of the romantic holiday image, but the secret of how it is done is simple. If you examine one of those still scenes closely, you will notice something missing. People. No, our picture postcard photographer did not take his pictures out of season. He just gets up early in the morning.

The picture postcard photographer, like the fishermen of the Costa Brava, knows full well that the early hours are the time when the sea is calm even though the sun is up. It is later in the day that the winds may come and spoil that lake-like surface inducing a nasty chop in a matter of minutes.

A choppy surface doesn't, of course, make spearfishing impossible – in fact for certain species of fish it provides ideal conditions – but it does make it less pleasant. It was for this reason that Francisco Castello would always stress the need for an early start to our week-end spearfishing trips with him and his friends.

So John and I would slip out of the still sleeping Murla Hotel and walk through the deserted Ramblas to the harbour. The air was fresh and clean at that time and though the sun was up it had a long way to go to reach the oven-intensity of midday and early afternoon.

Of course we were not the first up, and though most of the town seemed asleep – the Spaniards themselves slept late on Sunday mornings, but not so late as hung-over tourists – the water cart had already been around the streets leaving black patches in the dust and here and there a solitary figure would be wiggling a hosepipe around to lay more dust or wash clean the area in front of a hotel or restaurant.

Rendezvous point for our expeditions was the house of Juan Auladell, who together with his brother Bartholomew always took part in these fishing trips. The house, tall, grey and shuttered was on the front itself and only the wide earth stretches where the fishermen used to dry their nets separated it from the harbour wall.

John and I would look at the sea and sure enough as far as the eye could see, way past the harbour arm, out to the horizon and back to the headland of St Elmo, there was nothing but blue still water.

It was going to be a good day. We would put down the spearguns and the rest of our equipment and settle down to wait outside the house for the rest of them to turn up. It wasn't really very early. Francisco had said that we should meet at 8.30 a.m. sharp, but it would never be sharp as far as setting off was concerned.

At about a quarter to nine stirring noises and the smell of coffee would come from inside the house. Shutters would open and the tall figure of Juan would appear, mumbling something about having a cup of coffee.

At a few minutes to nine Francisco would round the corner from his house in the San Isidro with Julian, who worked for him and who would tend the boat while we spearfished. When Francisco arrived – he would jokingly call punctuality 'the English disease' – the expedition would get under way. First of all we would transfer all the equipment down to the beach where Francisco's boat, the *Santa Maria del Buen Ayre*, was kept hauled up out of the water.

Launching followed the reverse procedure for hauling the boat out. Heavy blocks of wood, greased in the centre to make the keel slide easily, were laid down in a pathway to the sea. We shoved; the boat moved down the sand. Blocks that were freed by this from under the bow were replaced under the keel at the stern until finally the boat was afloat.

Once in the water the hatches were taken off and one swing, after flooding the carburettor, was usually sufficient to bring the engine to thumping noisy life. It sounded shatteringly loud in the silence.

We always headed down the coast towards Tossa. First of all we would run through the narrow channel between Freu Island and St Elmo itself. There the engine's exhaust would come echoing back from the nearby rocks in staccato smacks of sound that contrasted strangely with the quieter thumping of the engine in the open sea.

Our route took us on down the coast, past Vigueta Bay with its steps hidden among the green and grey of the pines, past rose-pink cliffs that are the towering trademark of the Costa Brava and on to a point where the cliffs have collapsed so often that instead of being sheer they slope steeply, and vegetation, brambles and shrubs, have gained a foothold over the whole face. Here we would edge in towards the shore and the engine would be stopped long enough for the huge figure of Juan to enter the water.

31

At first, because this ritual was almost always the same, I thought that Juan made a point of swimming to the shore because the strong black Spanish coffee he had drunk for breakfast and the movement of the boat provided him with a natural laxative. I found out later that, though this was part of the reason, his main target was a great flat rock which had tumbled down in some fall of long ago and now lay half in the water on the boulder strewn beach. For some reason big bass liked that rock.

And Juan had taken several big fish by the technique of swimming in quietly from the sea and shooting the fish as they nosed around the rock in search of food.

Having dumped Juan the boat would move on. Julian, who took no part in the spearfishing but enjoyed himself hugely just looking after the boat, would wrinkle his face in mock disgust at the cigarette I offered him. He would say something in Catalan and point to his chest. I could catch the word *pulmones* as we struggled to understand one another. Lungs. Finally he would offer me one of his own cigarettes – hand-rolled and thick with black tobacco. I tried one once and was sure he was right. My commercially made cigarettes were certainly worse for the lungs than smoking his – no one in their right mind would even try to inhale the tobacco smoke that he enjoyed! I should of course have given up smoking after my chest trouble, but gradually got back into the habit.

Sometimes, these boat trips, would end in a barbecue on the beach – the taste of really fresh fish grilled on a flat tray of metal over a driftwood fire was superb, especially when washed down with wine from bottles which had been kept cool in the sea.

But there was one rule which was strictly observed. No women. Neither John's wife – nor mine when I married – were allowed in the boat. We tried to arrange it, but the disapproval was so evident that we dropped the matter.

I could never quite make out whether this was part of the old-fashioned Spanish belief that a women's place was not only in the home but also out of sight, or whether if they let one tourist friend's wife come, their wives would seize upon it as a lever to use for the emancipation of Spanish womanhood in general.

Not that there was even any risque conversation or anything like that. No. It was quite clear that there was no place for a woman on these fishing trips and that was that. A family outing was a different matter, but that was an exception to the rule and specially arranged.

The boat often stopped again not very far from where Juan had gone over the side. Then I would slip on an old sweat-shirt, for I had learnt the hard way what hours in the water can do when you combine it with the same length of time of Spanish sun on your back. Though you are never conscious of it at the time, the sun is at work in those moments between dives, when you are face down searching for likely spots. Then your back is just awash and the water cools it with every movement of either you or the sea. But the sun is getting through and many a novice spearfisherman or simple snorkeller watching the seabed life beneath him has ended with a badly burnt back.

So I put on my fins, tightened the cord of my swimming trunks, fixed knife belt and fish ring round my waist, spat in and washed out my mask, inhaled quickly through my nose to feel the mask grip with watertight seal on to my face, made sure that my loading pin was fastened to my wrist, put the snorkel mouthpiece in and then, with gun in one hand, slipped quietly over the side and into the cool of the sea.

The sea was often too deep at the point where I left the boat. You could tell at once. If the sea beneath me as I lay on the surface and started loading the gun, was a deep blue it would not matter even if I could see the bottom I knew it would be too deep for me.

I was never as good at deep diving as my Spanish friends. Sometimes when they glided along far below me and the sunlight made their bodies stand out light against the dark grey or black of the seabed rocks I would be deceived by the depth and start down to join them, but it was usually no good. I would use up too much air in clearing my ears and would have to stop and curve up to the surface leaving them some 20 feet below my deepest point.

So when the gun was loaded and the water was too deep, I headed in towards the shore in search of shallower water. For this reason I never shot a really big grouper there and missed, I suppose, the triumph of hauling one of those magnificent fish from its hole and boating it with fingers dug into its eye sockets for a proper grip.

Shallow water was, of course, instantly recognisable by the approach of the seabed, but even if you couldn't see the bottom I think I would recognise shallow Mediterranean water. It is blue, but not the deep blue further out. It has also a yellow tinge. This must be due to the reflection of sunlight from sand or light-coloured rocks, but is added to by the slight mistiness that comes from the suspended matter that there is bound to be close to any shore.

In those days 30 feet of water was quite enough to find large numbers of fish. Once I found myself in water that would not prove too exhausting – diving down again and again to look under rocks is very tiring – I would start to hunt. The secret of spearfishing is not travelling along the surface looking for signs of life and then diving down ready to fire. That is the novice's way and rarely results in much of a catch. The expert dives down first and then looks under every rock that he can. In fact he looks under the rock with his gun ready to fire, the moment his eyes have become accustomed to the gloom.

In the Mediterranean in the past even the novice's method would catch fish – for everywhere you looked from the surface there was movement.

Sars glittered silver in the sunlight and only on close approach would they flutter their black-banded tails and flee a zig-zag course. Sometimes they hid under a nearby rock and were an easy and obvious target. Everywhere the baby chromis fish, the black-and-purple 'flies of the sea' hung in clouds. Under big overhangs corbs would flutter their gorgeous fins like delicate veils around them and in and out of rock piles the spotted wrasse the French call *chenettes* would curl in and out of cover.

In 15 minutes of concentrated shooting you could fill the fish ring at your waist and then carry on hunting, looking for bigger and bigger fish.

One day I had reached this state and was working along the coast. I felt pleasantly tired and stopped to tread water and look around for the boat.

Though Julian's back was turned towards me and he was bent forward to cup his hands around a match for another of his diabolical cigarettes, it was comforting to see the boat was close enough not to have a long and exhausting swim when I decided to finish hunting.

I worked along a little further. Suddenly the rocks over which I had been swimming changed. The piled up boulders of the seabed gave way to one great flat sunlit rock. At the edge of this the water went deep blue and I was hanging over an abyss. It was beautiful. In the water hung clouds of 'sea flies'. Those closest to the surface looked purple and those below jet black. These little fish are usually fairly active, darting short distances this way and that without apparent reason. Now they were still, almost as if they too were just enjoying the view. Sunlight flickered down in bars of light and then petered out against the rich blue shading to black far below.

As I floated there watching, Juan joined the scene. Where he came from I don't know. I was too busy just sopping up the colours in my brain. But suddenly there he was 40 feet below me, drifting rather than finning along. At his approach the 'sea flies' parted and closed together again after him. He seemed so intent on something below him that I was convinced that he had spotted a big fish and was moving quietly after it. Somehow despite the long gun in his hand his figure did not intrude on the scene and I wished I had an underwater camera to record the colours and the peace of it all.

Later in the boat, I asked him what he had been chasing. 'Nothing,' he said, 'but wasn't it beautiful!' It is sights like these that 'hook' men and women on underwater swimming and take them back to the sea again and again.

Not that I needed hooking. I had been hooked for years. But my interest was changing. Changing so slowly that even I didn't really know what was happening. If you had asked me then if spearfishing was beginning to pall, I would have laughed at you. I would still have said that I thought it was the greatest sport of all.

Chapter
Three

My wife, Penny was a staff nurse at King's College Hospital. This you may think was a shrewd move to ensure instant medical attention. You could be wrong. She could swim like a fish and this meant that I would no longer be alone in my spearfishing forays!

I have never seen anyone take to a mask and fins the way that Penny did, and though the actual idea of spearing fish did not at first greatly appeal to her, I felt sure that she would soon become as enthusiastic as I was.

Our honeymoon took in all the places that I had wanted to go after reading spearfishing stories in diving magazines. We drove down through France in a Standard Ten, crossed into Spain near Hendaye, drove along ghastly 'tracks' to Bilbao and then plunged thankfully down through Portugal on their magnificent roads. Magnificent that is, compared with the pot-holed thumping we had taken along the Atlantic coast of Spain.

In the North of Portugal we found out something that even today the tourist guides will do their best to conceal from you. That however hot are the magnificent sands of Northern Portugal – and they are wonderful sandy beaches without doubt and the sun scorches down – the sea is absolutely freezing. This is not to say that in freak years the sea is not kinder, but to make it clear that generally the water is so cold that if you plunge in without knowing, you float for a moment stunned with what can only described as a headache clamped in an iron band round the level of your temples.

But don't be put off. The eating is superb, the people charming, but if you want to splash in warmer seas head South. The low temperature of the sea in the North is, I am assured, only a contrast with the warmth on shore, but you have been warned.

Even in 1955 we were objects of curiosity to the locals and swimming in the great rollers near Nazare brought entire villages out to line the beach in solemn black and watch these strange creatures who actually swam in the sea for fun.

The spearfishing was good. I know now that I didn't sample the best of it for we were itching to get to the far South. Even so the hospitality of the people of Portugal was impossible to forget. Penny was taught to play the *fado* on guitar and I to drink wines that I never dreamed existed.

It seems funny to write this now. The wines that were almost unobtainable in this country then were the green wines – the Vinho Verdes – that are sisters to Mateus Rose. They prickled on our tongues and we thought we had found something that very few Britons would ever taste unless they ventured into Portugal. Now the descendants of the wines we drank are commonplace in every decent off-licence and sold in many a steak-house.

We had decided to drive right round the sea coast of Spain and Portugal. So we pushed through what is now the Portuguese tourist boomland of the Argarve, spearfished at Cadiz, saw the apes in Gibraltar, watched the most fantastic flamenco at a farm near Seville and stopped in a tourist town called Torremolinos. The hotels were already there, but following the directions of a helpful hotel reception desk clerk we headed back to Marbella and found a completely deserted beach and headland all to ourselves.

Those who know the package tour paradise of Torremolinos today will find this impossible to visualise – as well they might. But there is not really any truth in the story that General Franco having seen what happened to Torremolinos and its surroundings from the vantage point of his yacht on a coastal cruise ordered that such a thing must never happen again to any stretch of the Spanish coastline. Though if it had been true, that would have been one justification for a dictatorship!

But this was long ago and there we were in the blazing sunshine with sand too hot to walk on with bare feet, no one else in sight and a clump of off-shore rocks within easy swimming distance in a sea that bounced the sunlight painfully into the eyes.

And if you find it impossible to visualise a beach near

37

Torremolinos without people you will also find it impossible to believe that there, in that clump of off-shore rocks, we found big groupers. Even then those groupers were no fools. They would hang tail down, head up watching our approach with obvious curiosity. At the head-on dive that I tried first time to get within firing range of these fine fish they turned and belted for the cover of the holes they called home.

But curiosity is the downfall of the grouper inside diveable range. If you return to the surface for air and then dive down once again to the entrance to the hole and wait outside until your lungs are bursting and your mask is stuck tight to your face as you inhale even the air that is inside, the grouper is likely to look out to see what is going on. A shot through the head is not then difficult.

A killing shot is essential. Because if you fail with that first shot and the grouper has time to return to its hole, you will spend dive after dive trying to extract the fish from its hiding place.

What happens is this. The fish has a habit of erecting all its fins inside the confined space of the hole and will continue to do so until death does its part. In fact some really big specimens will die in position and resist all efforts to tear them out into the open sea even when life has long departed.

This is the reason for those wide-mouthed gaffs, whose great steel hooks and rubber-encased handles are still to be seen in shops in Spain that specialise in goods for the underwater swimmer. Only the use of something like that can tear out the fish, which though mortally wounded, has fixed itself into position in a deep-down hole.

I didn't have this trouble on the Torremolinos coast but I was considerably miffed when returning proudly with my fish ring to the hotel the hotel clerk dismissed my catch as too small to cook. 'Some French divers,' he said sniffily, 'last week had some real fish.' I was so cross that I walked straight out of the hotel and gave them to the nearest Spaniard I could find. As he had just arrived at the hotel to unload a mass of wine bottles he was completely mystified at this unexpected, but welcome, present. Though his gratitude was somewhat mollifying, Torremolinos, for me, then lost any charm that it might have had.

So we pushed on. With a short stop at Malaga to see Litri fight his last bull (and hardly go out in a blaze of glory though he returned to the ring later) we headed for Granada (to see the palace) and then down the most incredibly winding road to Motril and the coast once again.

Motril. Every spearfishing article and book I had read had stressed that this was the real home of the grouper. Giant groupers, the authors had written, were there for the taking in the water directly under those precipitous cliffs.

The precipitous cliffs were there all right – the road clung to them in a series of hair-raising hairpins – but one thing that none of the articles had mentioned was the difficulty of getting down to the sea. I tried to rent a boat in the few little ports along the coast but had no luck. It was infuriating. There was the sea – and the only thing that separated me from it was just a few hundred feet of sheer cliff.

I got so desperate that the next time we crossed a small bridge, covering a steep winter water-course that led down to the sea I managed at the risk of a scraped wing to nudge the car into a position that would cause no hazard to any other traffic. Then Penny and I, carrying the minimum of spear-fishing gear, clambered down the river-bed to sea-level.

We emerged on a tiny beach which had been made by the rubble brought down by winter rains. I entered the water sure that now real spearfishing was about to begin. It was one of the greatest disappointments of my life. Not only were there no giant groupers; there were no fish of any kind. All the rocks were covered with the white 'flowers' of pavonia – I have noticed since that the presence of these growths in quantity usually means no fish – and the whole bay appeared to be almost sterile. I can't explain this. The whole area seemed dead and we clambered up again in the sweaty heat without the slightest thing to show for our efforts.

After that I'm afraid we abandoned the South of Spain and made a beeline back for the place that I knew best – San Feliu de Guixols on the Costa Brava.

San Feliu was much more crowded. Package tours had brought the tourists in full force. There were fewer fish to be seen on spearfishing hunts. In memory it all seems to have happened at once, but of course it didn't. Memory has a trick of telescoping events together and in fact the fish had gradually become fewer over the years.

John Messent was as keen on spearfishing as ever. He abandoned Spanish waters and came back from Yugoslavia with tales of monstrous fish seen and shot. His brother Robin, who had often joined us spearfishing in Spain, had been on holiday with the Club Mediterranee and had started using an aqualung.

Penny and I climbed down to Vigueta and she tried her hand at spearfishing with a small gun with trident headed spear. But after she nearly shot a giant moray eel – all yellow and orange spots down the length of its brown body – and I only just managed to stop her in time, she reverted to watching sea life not killing it.

I'm glad she didn't manage to shoot that moray. The water was only a few feet deep and the reaction of such a large fish – it was several feet long – was reasonably easy to forecast !

Though the no-women rule was not relaxed, thereby giving Penny plenty of time for window shopping while we were gone, something had changed too about Francisco's spearfishing trips. Now a big brown box would be carefully loaded into the boat.

It contained a large yellow-bottled aqualung and after the spearfishing was over, Francisco would go for a cruise around by himself. I hardly thought of this as dangerous at the time. Francisco was such a strong swimmer and expert spearfisherman that it never occurred to me – I suppose I knew; perhaps I didn't – that he was breaking the cardinal diving rule by diving alone.

The reason for taking the lung to the boat in the box was, they said, so that his wife would not get upset about him using the aqualung.

Later on, Spain made a law that spearfishing with aqualungs was illegal and that no boat was allowed to carry both lungs and guns. One or the other, but not both together. The penalty for doing so was harsh. At the least it meant confiscation of boat and all equipment. That law, a sensible one in my opinion, is in force today as it is in many countries. Without such a rule there would be no groupers left down to 200 feet. They are difficult enough to find now in depths under 100 feet anywhere near the more popular tourist areas.

So Francisco had his aqualung. Robin Messent was talking about having used one. And I had scorned them after that one short stay on the tiled floor of a swimming pool in Chelsea. I still cannot imagine why diving with compressed air had not appealed to me at once, but it didn't and even then I didn't seem to be taking much interest. It was still spearfishing for me.

Fish were getting more difficult to find and to shoot but that didn't mean that you couldn't. In fact on one of the boat trips with my Spanish friends, I got myself a nice 6 lb. bass. Not a big fish by spearfishing record standards, but very nice eating.

I had been working along the stretch of coast that we had covered so often in the past when I came to Juan's flat rock. As I finned gently up to it, a great silver fish exploded into flight almost directly in front of me. I fired far too late and the spear fell away to clank on the shallow bottom feet behind the fish's fast fanning tail.

Reeling in my spear and reloading I called myself all sorts of idiots for not being on the alert and swam, without hurrying, over the ridge in the same direction as the bass had gone. The water was shallow and I had no thought of seeing the bass again, when, to my amazement, I saw, poking out from a flat rock in the middle of a gully, a huge tail. It was my bass.

I didn't wait to ask why the bass should take shelter in such a place instead of heading out to the open sea – there was nothing to bar his way – but dived down and estimating where the body of the fish was, planted the harpoon solidly into his side. The next seconds were literally a whirl of activity. The fish shot out of his hiding place and swam round and round me to the limit of the line free from the reel and attached to the harpoon.

I could see that the spear was not through the fish and would not stand much more of this activity before pulling out and letting the fish escape. After four or five of these revolutions with me spinning round like a top in the centre, the fish's strength gave out. It flopped to the rocks on its side. This gave me the chance to fin forward and push the spear right through its body by hand.

I was in the boat with my catch safe and sound when Juan

returned. He didn't need telling where I had got it. He knew it was from his rock.

I was proud of my catch and even more so when it was borne to our table in the Murla dining-room on a silver dish for dinner that night. Josef Murla had cooked it intact and propped its mouth open with a whole tomato. It seemed a shame to break into it, but it was delicious. When we could eat no more the remainder was taken back to the kitchen.

'Did you enjoy it?' asked Josef later.

'Yes, thank you,' I said, 'it was delicious.'

'You left the best part,' he said with a grin.

And then he explained, as I vaguely remember Lola Kristo explaining to me years ago in France, that gourmets believe that the most tasty part of any fish is the flesh from the two depressions 'behind the ears'. Though I can understand that, I have never quite been able to understand the behaviour of that bass.

Several spearfishing experts who have taken bass in both the Mediterranean and British waters have suggested that the Mediterranean bass may be a slightly different species to that found around our own coasts. They quote similar experiences to mine in the Med. but never quite so blatant a conceal-ment. In their experiences the bass sought cover as almost a last resort when the route to the open sea was blocked. Mine had nothing to stop him from heading out to North Africa if he so wished.

Fish experts will not accept the theory that Mediterranean bass are any different from the bass of Britain, though they say that fish of course adapt to their environment and adopt different behaviour patterns in different waters.

In Britain bass usually adopt the pattern of instant flight to the open sea when confronted with a diver or spearfisher-man. Though John Messent did on one occasion find a big bass that he thought had gone for ever, apparently hiding from him in thick weeds.

For our next year's holiday we decided to try somewhere else. Penny was pregnant and after circling round Swiss hospitals for some time we decided that this cautious attitude was ridic-ulous and pointed the car's nose towards Sicily. Surely the spearfishing there would be marvellous?

We drove down the East coast of Italy spearfishing without much success – at least I was still spearfishing though Penny, who was seven months into pregnancy took only gentle dips into the water – until we reached Brindisi. Then we cut across the Heel to Taranto and finally ended up on the car ferry at Reggio di Calabria bound for Messina.

On Sicily the spearfishing was good and though it was only May the hillsides were already burnt brown by the sun. But it wasn't the heat that I really remember, but the three frights I got during our stay on the island. Fear never seems far away from me in the underwater world, but the first of these frights had nothing to do with the sea.

We had stopped at a little trattoria for lunch. It really was an idyllic spot overlooking the sea far below. Inside it was cool and great wine butts lined one of the whitewashed walls. We lunched simply but well – and I made a great discovery. I found out what the Romans and Greeks, whose temples studded the island, were writing about when they described a wine as 'nectar of the gods'. The white wine – to be accurate it had a slightly yellowish glow – that we had with the meal was like nothing I had ever tasted before. It had something of a Lachrymae Christi about it, but it was much much more. It was obviously the nectar of the gods.

The wine came from one of the great barrels on the far wall and the method of serving it was simply to hold an empty bottle under the tap and then bring it without cork to the table. I thought it was great, Penny thought it was great and so I called for another bottle. At this moment a man who had been sitting eating his lunch several tables away said quietly, in French: 'Faites attention, c'est tres fort.' I thanked him, but thought his advice ridiculous. It was more like grape juice than wine.

Within seconds I had cause to regret that decision. Without a word of warning Penny crashed face-downwards on the table. She was out cold. I shoved my handkerchief into the water jug and tried applying the sopping rag to the back of her neck, but it had no effect. Suddenly I was pushed aside by at least three Sicilian women who carried the limp form of Penny out of the dining area through a curtain into the back of the little restaurant. When I attempted to follow I was given what was obviously a lecture about the effect of wine on pregnant women judging by the number of times 'vino' and 'bambino' appeared in the torrent of words that were poured crossly at me.

The woman was right, the Frenchman was right – and I was a fool. When I finally managed to break away and pass the curtain I was vastly relieved to see Penny was conscious. She managed a weak grin from a deck-chair which supported her back while her feet were propped high in the air on a pile of old boxes. I was then lectured by each of the three women in turn until Penny felt strong enough to leave. As we drove away I knew that the Frenchman had been right if only by the splitting headache that hit me almost as soon as I stepped into the blazing sunshine.

I didn't repeat that stupidity again – in fact it was as much as Penny could do to get me to allow her a sip of wine at meals.

My second fright however did come from the sea. I was snorkelling among the little rocks close inshore near a Sicilian village. It was very pretty underwater – in fact I spent ages following a little sea-horse around as it fanned its way along in an upright position from weed-patch to weed-patch. Finally I lost it in a big clump of weeds. There its camouflage was so complete that once having taken my eyes off it I could not find it again, though it must have been within inches of my mask at some time during my search.

I decided to explore a reef that ran out from the shore to a large clump of black rocks. In a way this reef formed a natural harbour for the two or three small fishing boats drawn up on the shore and the rocks at the end formed a small island that marked the harbour's entrance.

My exploration was not particularly quiet or careful. I saw one or two fish but nothing of a size that seemed worth shooting. As I rounded the end rock on the inside of the islet, I was already thinking about swimming back to the stony beach from which I had come.

It was getting late and the sun was losing its penetration through the water. As a result it appeared to be getting a little misty, though whether this was entirely due to the lower angle of the sun or whether it was the result of my approach to the open sea I didn't even bother to think. Certainly the water round the island deepened.

Then I saw it! At least I saw its eye. A gigantic thing like a football with a great black centre. I looked right into it. We were eyeball to eyeball and the eye of the thing was cold. My heart juddered and tried to jump off its mountings. I started to turn in a frantic effort to get away and as I did so something blue-grey in the water behind the eye moved too. Something so big that all the water wasn't water but a blue-grey thing. Then the eye was gone and the water heaved against me and I was well on my way back to the beach. I don't know what it was. But the tunny traps a little further along the coast made me think that a big tunny and I had been face to face for just a few seconds.

I can kid myself now that if the thing had stayed only a second longer I would have shot it, but I know that the thought never entered my head. All I wanted to do at the time was to get away.

The tunny traps provided me with Fright Number 3. I had arranged with an old fisherman of a village from which the tunny nets stretched out to the open sea, to take me out to see them. At five a.m. he was waiting and Penny and I embarked.

He must have been over 70, but the only motive power for the boat was a pair of oars and his arms. He rowed and rowed and rowed until I felt bound to ask in sign language if I could take over for a while. He accepted with alacrity and slowly – more slowly than when he was rowing – we worked our way out along the endless line of buoys towards the heart of the traps. My stint at the oars was fortunately not too long because a passing much bigger fishing boat with an engine – taking the men out to the traps – chucked us a line and took us in tow.

Near the actual traps we were cast off and completed the remaining distance under oar power. The tunny trapping system was the same then as it obviously had been for centuries. The tunny make their annual migration along the shores of Sicily and always swim – at least so I understood my fisherman to say – with one eye on the coastline. When they see the single net stretching out from the shore, they are believed to assume that this is an extension of the coast and so they turn and follow it along.

This habit proves fatal for the net leads into a series of

net chambers, all are open ended except for the last. This is the *chambre del morte*. Once the tunny are inside that in sufficient quantities to justify the labour involved the shore entrance is closed and the bottom is slowly hauled up until the whole net is a solid thrashing mass of fish.

Then the fishermen go to work with gaffs and other implements. Anything, judging from the collection of weapons I saw, will do as long as it is hooked and can be stuck into the fish. There was even a rusty hand scythe!

As we rowed into the net complex, the old fisherman called out to the capo or chief fisherman for 'permissione' to enter the netted area. I was impressed with the respect that the old man paid to the chief, but I found out later that the word of the captain of the tunny trap is law. And you can understand it. The village's prosperity obviously depended on a good catch.

Permission having been granted we rowed into the centre of the nets. This was no flimsy temporary set up, but included boardwalks along the sides and at one point two men squatted on a board that ran across the entrance to the net traps. From their fingers dangled thin weighted lines. The old man asked them something as we passed and they shook their heads. Apparently by this method of thin lines running down across the entrance to the trap they can tell exactly how many tunny are inside from the knocks on the lines – and the exact moment when the run starts.

It seemed a pretty ghastly job to me. Though the sun was not yet high, I could imagine what squatting there in the full glare of a Sicilian heatwave, which we seemed to be in at the time, would be like.

Fright number 3 was rushing up on me, but I didn't know it. All I was aware of was a rapid exchange of what I took to be jokes, judging from the grins on the faces of all concerned, between my old fisherman guide and the waiting tunnymen.

A few moments later the old man indicated that as there were no tunny around I might care to inspect the trap using my mask. I didn't exactly jump at the chance, but as it was not my policy to refuse a new experience, I put it on and slipped into the water. And Fright number 3 exploded in my face.

Right in front of me were the great brown-black bars of the netting, but more important than that was the fact that

I was face to face with a shark. A shark inside the net with mouth wide open and the finest display of teeth that you ever did see.

I practically walked on the water and was back in the boat almost before I had left it. Penny's face registered alarm at the sight of my face, but the tunny-fishermen nearly had hysterics. In fact they laughed so much that one of them nearly fell off the boardwalk. The old man was grinning like a Sicilian Cheshire cat – and I realised that they had known the shark was there all the time.

It was big but harmless. I only realised this when the old man produced a glass-bottomed tin and let me look through it. The shark was dead, drowned when the net had held its gills open. This was the reason for the gaping mouth. I had recovered a little now and tried one or two pictures through the tin. In fact I tried to laugh with the fishermen and they hauled the shark out to show me.

Sharks apparently follow the tunny, but this one was ahead of the mob. The fisherman had another reason for hauling out the dead shark. They believe that the presence of any dead fish will disturb the tunny.

An oily swell was now making the water move after the dead calm of dawn and Penny began to feel seasick, something to which it seems she is only prone when pregnant. The fishermen were all kindness and offered her some kind of fizzy coffee-flavoured drink which worked like a charm, but there seemed no point in staying at the traps any longer. The fish, said the fishermen, would not run that day now.

The next day we moved on – so I never had the opportunity of seeing the massacre of the tunny. Perhaps it is just as well. I don't think either of us would have liked it. The sea turns red with blood and the killing is merciless. Not that one can blame tunnymen for this. The tunny's death gives them life.

I talked to Ley Kenyon, one of Britain's most experienced diving cameramen, about this trip to the tunny traps and he tells me that he has actually filmed inside the 'death chamber' when it was full of tunny and the net was being hauled up.

He had feared before the actual event that he would be severely battered by the trapped fish as they dashed that way

47

and this in an attempt to escape. In fact he told me that even when the area of the net still in the water seemed too small to hold all the fish and himself the huge tunny never touched him even when passing within fractions of an inch. He finally left the water only because the captain of the nets ordered him out as he feared that Ley himself would be gaffed by a fisherman in the confusion!

The next year we went back to Spain. Before that, of course Penny had given me a son, Kevin. He weighed 9 lb. 9 oz. – but we have no means of knowing how much the Sicilian wine contributed to that fine weight! At any rate we decided that he would be quite happy with my sister, Christine, at her home in Westerham while we snatched a quick holiday abroad.

Even though we were not away for long, something happened on that holiday which was the first sign that I was coming to the end of my spearfishing.

I was in Vigueta bay on a normal spearfishing foray. The shortage of fish had become most noticeable and so I was well pleased to find a big fat corb under a rock. I dived and made no mistake. The fish was pierced right through and I dragged it fluttering and kicking up after me to the surface.

As I grabbed the end of the harpoon preparatory to transferring the fish to my fish ring, it looked at me. I can't describe what it was about that particular fish which triggered off my pity. But two gobbets of blood glowed in the water against the pale blue background of distant visibility and the sunlight struck the fish and it still looked at me. And well, it looked so sad.

I thought about letting it go, but that would have been even more cruel for the spear had badly damaged it. So I killed it quickly with my knife and remembered the words of a friend who said: 'When you think about it, it must be like shoving a telegraph pole through a man – from the point of view of size that is . . .'

I can still remember that fish. And I still feel unhappy about it. But why that one and why not all the others?

The next year we decided to try somewhere different again. So we went to Sardinia. In an old Dakota, christened for brochure purposes a 'Dakmaster' we staggered across France and out over the sea. From the air Sardinia looked a spearfisherman's paradise and my hopes were high. Even a quick dip in the sea near the hotel did not dampen them. The barren condition of the seabed was, I thought, only to be expected so close to a well-populated shore.

Kevin was with us on this holiday and Penny was pregnant with Joanna, but we hired a little Fiat and drove about exploring the north of the island. We were probably unlucky in the spots we chose for swimming, but there seemed to be remarkably few fish about. The shortage was explained when I came across a series of what could only be described as small craters blown in the seabed.

It took some time to find out that one of the local methods of fishing seemed to be the use of dynamite. This was, of course, strictly against the law and I was told that a nasty incident had happened only a month or two previously when the carabineri had caught two fishermen in the act of lobbing dynamite into the water. The carabineri had called on the fishermen to stop, but one of them in the middle of throwing the bomb had continued his arm action – not surprising as the fuse was already burning – in the direction of the police.

They had opened fire and one of the fishermen had been killed. Local feeling was so aroused by this that the carabineri concerned had been hastily transferred off the island.

I was sure that there was, however, good spearfishing to be had if it were possible to use a boat and get out along the rocky shores. The opportunity came when an excursion to some caves with boat trip was advertised. The boat skipper seemed much in favour of a spot of spearfishing and agreed to let me off at a promising spot.

The scenery away from the populated areas was magnificent and I spent a happy hour working around some offshore rocks under huge cliffs. But apart from one large bass my total catch was disappointing. I'm sure, though, that had I been a better diver the deeper water would have paid off handsomely. It all looked so splendid with ravines and overhangs and glorious blue water. But it was all very deep.

We enjoyed the holiday – more for the sights of the island than the spearfishing – and can still remember tearing through what local residents assured us was bandit country following a priest on a motor-cycle who was guiding us to the nuraghi, the Stone Age dwellings that sit mysteriously out in open country.

The priest drove at a hair-raising pace and it was all that the little Fiat could do to keep up. With the skirts of his cassock billowing dangerously around the back wheel, he must certainly have believed in Divine Providence!

One word of warning to parents who intend to take young children to Sardinia – the Italians (Sardinian variety) dote on youngsters, particularly rosy-cheeked English toddlers. After any trip down a shopping street we used to have to empty Kevin out. Not only his mouth, but his pockets would be stuffed full of sweets put there in handfuls by the proprietors of any shop he passed!

The next year we were back in Spain again. And my spear-fishing days were over. Though I didn't know it, they were over the moment I saw a Land Rover in the streets of San Feliu. It had large noticeboards on the sides. They read : 'Anglo-Spanish Undersea School' and added the offer of diving lessons.

I pointed the Land Rover out to Penny as it went past. 'I'd like to try that,' I said. 'Why don't you,' she replied, 'and if it doesn't cost too much, I'd like to have a go too.'

Chapter
Four

Pat and Joan Harrison were the Anglo-Spanish Undersea School. And we found them in the Club's headquarters, a second-floor flat in one of the side roads off the narrow main shopping streets of San Feliu.

Pat looked the part of a rugged diver. A craggy face was topped by a mass of white curly hair giving him the right sea-dog impression. He had, I gathered, been many things in life – Marine Commando, prisoner-of-war (during which time his hair had gone white), boxer, judo instructor, swimming bath superintendent, and commercial diver. He and Joan were now trying to make a commercial success of running a diving school.

Both were extremely talkative. But whereas Pat's talk was mostly of diving, Joan was the expert on what went on in the town, where to buy this and that and who was the right person to see if you wanted something made specially for you.

Underwater equipment littered the flat and the atmosphere was much more friendly than businesslike. In fact the nearest we got to business details was that we should meet the next day on the rocks at Port Salvi. More sherry was sloshed into tumblers and some sort of price was mentioned. I think it was 100 pesetas a dive – not bad when this figure included all equipment, air and instruction.

I know that my ambition at that time was to dive to 100 feet. Robin Messent had talked airily of this sort of thing taking place during his Club Mediterranee holiday and I didn't want to be left behind.

To my surprise Pat Harrison didn't think reaching this depth would involve a great deal of training as I had done a fair amount of spearfishing. Whether it was this prospect or the sherry, I know that I left the flat with Penny very taken with the whole idea of learning to dive with an aqualung.

We met as arranged the next morning. Port Salvi Cove was, said Pat, much deeper than you would think. Close to the rocks of course it was shallow, but it shelved steeply downward.

I was all impatience to get in the water and start, but Pat Harrison was obviously not going to be rushed. If I was in such a hurry to get off the hot rocks, he suggested that I should go for a snorkelling trip first. He lay down on the rocks and seemed disinclined to do anything else but chat.

I picked up my mask, fins, snorkel tube and speargun and headed for the water followed by the shouted instructions of Joan Harrison not to dare shoot her pet squid or pet octopus which lived under some rocks nearby. Both she and Pat had a strong objection to spearfishing, but I was so keen to learn to dive that I didn't bother to argue with them.

I suspected that Pat Harrison wanted to see me in the water to make his own assessment of my capabilities, so I swam some distance out and decided to do some serious fishing. I found almost immediately that what he had said about Port Salvi Cove was true. Only a short way out I couldn't reach the bottom and so my spearfishing was rather limited.

Pat seemed satisfied, for, on my return, the rocks turned into a classroom and I was carefully taught about the first principles of diving. Then we took to the shallow water. It was much easier than I thought and my main concern was not to hold my breath as all my earlier spearfishing training had taught me. We practiced mask clearing – and tube clearing (we were using the old Siebe Gorman demand valves which had none of the modern non-return valves in the mouthpiece and flooded tubes were a serious inconvenience).

And then we took a short trip down into the depths and back again. Looking back now the depth was hardly likely to have been more than 40 feet, but it seemed deep at the time.

They say that each pupil hero-worships his first instructor. That may be true. There is no doubt that after spending some time in the water with Pat Harrison I had a great respect for his capabilities.

My tuition did not finish with the end of the dive. The aqualung bottles had to be filled and in those early days there was no compressor in San Feliu and we had to drive into

Gerona to get the bottles filled. This took most of the late afternoon and evening when combined with a shopping trip in the cool arcade under the arches of the main shopping street.

I haven't been into Gerona for some years, but even now I can remember the smell of rotting material which rose from the river as it passed through the centre of the town. In fact if you say Gerona to me – that's the thought that still springs to mind.

The next few days – and the end of our holiday was coming up fast – were spent in a steady routine.

At 11 a.m. we met on the rocks. An hour later we would start diving. And we managed to find enough cash for Penny to have a go too. Which when I think about it meant that she didn't get much of a share of the diving. Most of her time was spent swimming over our bubbles or sitting baking on the rocks.

Lunch came about 3 p.m. on the patio of the Murla with its plants in pots and vines twisting up the supports of the awning and flowers everywhere. Then siesta until six. Then drinks and a stroll round town. Then dinner about 11 p.m. And then brandies and coffee with Pat and Joan, either at the hotel or at some little bar they knew in town.

But even then the 'day' wasn't over. Often in the cool of the early hours we would still be playing 'bowls' – a primitive version of today's ten-pin bowling with cement alleys, great chipped wooden balls, battered skittles and little Spanish boys setting up the pins and hurling the balls back down the 'gutters'.

The alley was on the front right by the harbour wall. Behind the alley was a thatched roof and a little bar and tables and chairs. But it's all gone now. Swept away in the tourist rush on the grounds that 'it was creating too much noise'.

Even in those early days you still had to wait for a chance to play and I suppose that it could never have coped with today's mass tourism. But I don't remember all that amount of noise – perhaps the occasional drunken shout of triumph, but usually all you could hear was a hum of conversation superimposed on the rumble of wood over cement and the hollow clop of ball striking ball when returned or the thunk of ball striking pin.

Keeping these late hours meant that the late start to our

diving in the morning was sensible. And in the sheltered cove of Salvi it didn't matter that we missed the calm seas of the early morning.

As our holiday came towards its end I began to wonder whether I would ever manage the magic 'ton'. The deepest I had been so far was 60 feet over a great carpet of thin green 'eel-grass' or posidonia weed that sloped gently downwards into the mist of depth. I felt I was ready for 100 feet. We had done a great deal of training including a frustrating session using a surface demand set-up. This meant that you were still breathing compressed air from a cylinder, but in this case the demand valve that supplied you with the correct pressure of air for the depth was separated from the air bottle by yards and yards of rubber high-pressure hose.

You wore a harness like an aqualung harness, but only the demand valve was mounted on your back by it. From the valve away went the hose up to the surface and a huge bottle of compressed air jammed in a cleft in the rocks.

It was frustrating because you could swim only in a circle dictated by the length of the hose. It was all part of Pat Harrison's familiarisation training and has a mass of uses in commercial and other diving which required work at a special spot on the seabed, or, when the compressor or air supply was in a boat, long periods underwater at shallow depth.

Finally my chance came. The next day was to be our last and Pat had agreed to take me down to 100 feet. I don't know why I was so obsessed by this desire for depth. It happens with all novice divers and they are usually disappointed – there is much more life in shallower water. But practically every young diver wants to be able to boast about 'over 100 feet, old man' and I don't suppose all the wise words in the world will change that side of human nature.

The weather was distinctly off when we met the next morning. The sea outside the bay was quite lumpy, there was a wind and even the sheltered waters of the cove were beginning to stir. Pat, as usual, wasn't in any hurry to dive. He looked at the sky, strolled off to talk to some other people on the rocks and left me in a fever of impatience.

Finally, I asked him point-blank: 'What's the matter? Don't you want to dive?' The question stung him for some reason.

'Get your gear on,' he snapped. Joan said something about it being too rough – and waves were beginning to sweep around the sides of the cove. But we went ahead.

The dive itself was uneventful. I swam side by side with Pat down over the sun-dappled whitish rocks of the shallows which I knew so well from our training sessions, down over the green weed and then at a steeper angle over black rocks to the sand. The sunlight had gone now and the light was grey – grey sand, darker grey – almost black rocks and a sort of grey glow over everything. Suddenly Pat reached out and gripped my wrist. I jumped and then saw that he was putting our depth-gauges side by side. Both read over 30 metres. We were already over the 100 foot mark. I was surprised and yes, a little disappointed. I looked round. It was distinctly dull. We started back more slowly than we had come. I felt cold and the thin sweat-shirt I wore seemed to provide no warmth at all.

Yet to be honest though the view at 100 feet had been disappointing I did have a sense of achievement. Soon we were back in depths where you could see the surface. But it wasn't the glistening mirror that I had grown accustomed to. This was a greyer surface and when I broke through it I knew why. The sun still shone but the sea inside the bay was distinctly rough. By timing the right moment Pat got out easily and then stretched a hand back for me.

'Thank you,' I said to him. 'I'm sorry you were cross with me when we went in . . .'

'I wasn't worried about getting in,' he said, 'any fool can get in, it's the getting out that can be difficult. Still its not too bad . . .'

The waves were getting up though and I wouldn't like to have been coming out by the time we looked back after packing up all the gear and climbing up the rocks. Pat grinned and said : 'You know its a funny thing, nobody stays cross with anyone else for long underwater !'

And you know he is right. I had felt his anger when we went in, but within a few moments of starting down I was also conscious of the fact that the anger had evaporated.

The relationship between a diver and his regular partner is a special one. But it is not just the closeness of two people

55

who have accomplished some fairly hazardous task and feel therefore a special relationship. It is, of course, to some extent a friendship which demands trust and is not let down.

It is a unique situation which they share. There is no noise, no exchange of words to convey feelings or exchange impressions. They are together, a team, in a thick world of silence. Sometimes I think that divers experience the beginnings of the same sort of communication relationship underwater which obviously exists among a school of certain tiny fish. All turn the same way at once; all changes of direction are conveyed instantaneously through the whole school no matter how big. Somehow information is conveyed from one fish to another.

Of course divers don't all change direction at the same time no matter how often they dive together. But there is this feeling of closeness and understanding without words.

I'm sure there is a perfectly logical explanation of the sharpening of the senses that comes from the mere fact of being underwater – and here I am not talking about diving to great depths because, of course, there a dulling of the senses takes place.

In the same way, just as I was conscious of anger at the beginning of my first deep dive, its evaporation, and a sense of well-being on return to the surface, there must be a logical explanation of the sense of euphoria that usually comes to a diver on return to the surface.

I once heard a commentator to an underwater film refer to the fact that the divers sat silent in the boat after their dive 'because they were stunned by the beauty of what they had seen'. I offered to posterity at the time a substitute phrase for his future use – 'because they were stunned by the fact that they were still alive'. Neither, of course, is true. A diving boat after a dive is a buzz of 'Did you see that . . . ? 'So close I could have touched it . . .' and 'God, it must have been at least . . .'

So whether my feeling of some sort of mental communication between divers is true or not, there is not the slightest doubt that divers on returning to shore or boat enjoy a feeling of happiness and an eagerness to exchange impressions of things seen during their stay below. It is very rare to find a bad-tempered diver *after* a dive. All sorts of things may have gone wrong, but basically I have always felt that if they do the expressions of anger from the returning diver have a sort of mock fury.

This is not to say that it is not possible to feel fury or frustration while down below. Of course it is. But it is my experience that such things do not survive the joy of surfacing and however deeply felt at the time rarely exist after the dive as more than cause for a joke.

However, all these things hardly affected me at this time. I had switched over to the aqualung. Spearfishing seemed a bit old hat.

Bromley Branch was my local British Sub-Aqua Club branch and so I presented myself at Downham Baths and started in again from the beginning. But I didn't mind. I just kicked myself for being so stupid all those years ago.

At any rate the beginning was where I needed to begin. Pat Harrison had taught me well; I was happy about that. But there were more things I needed to know to equip myself to dive in British waters.

I soon realised that I knew practically nothing at all about that. This is not to belittle the training that Pat Harrison had given me, but I had not given him enough time to bring me right up to date on the state of the art.

Looking back in my log-book I see that on the 14th of November, 1959 I passed the swimming test – Group A. It was the day after my birthday. I was 32 and so that I could start training I had to swim 100 yards freestyle, 50 yards backstroke, and 50 yards any stroke wearing a ten-pound weightbelt. I floated on my back for five minutes. I trod water with my hands above my head for one minute and I recovered six objects from the deep end of the training pool – the objects were lead weights off a weightbelt – without difficulty.

I don't propose to write down the B.S.A.C. schedule of training here, but it included lectures on and questioning about anoxia, ears and sinuses, surfacing drill, protective clothing, principles of the aqualung, air embolism, air endurance, and practical tests in fitting all equipment underwater.

We sloshed, waterlogged, away from the pool to the 'dry meeting' as they called them – strange for the title of any meeting held in a pub – and happily got signatures in our log-book for those tests passed.

There are still fools around today who decry the British Sub-Aqua Club's standards of training. In grand manner these fools declare that the Club's system is all tests and lectures and that the really true test of a diver is the way that he handles himself in the sea.

And they are quite right. But a diver has little or no chance of handling himself properly in the sea unless he has a grasp of the principles behind what he is doing and enough confidence in his equipment – gained only by experience in swimming pools and calm waters – to use it and not abuse it. Any fool can swim about in the sea as long as everything goes right. It's when things go wrong that you can sort out the trained diver from the bloke who thinks all tests are a load of tripe.

Bromley Branch of the B.S.A.C. was, I am glad to say, not prepared to sign up log-books or tests passed just on the word of the trainee. But they had got one nasty habit that I didn't find out about until after one particular watery session which involved fitting all equipment underwater without surfacing.

A massive fair-haired man was taking the test at the same time. This was Malcolm Todd and he provided the spur of competition that I needed to get me through the tests. He was much better at everything concerned with the water than I was so I never had a chance to relax. He was also – which was to prove vastly useful in the years to come – an expert metallurgist and the kind of man who could build a compressor from a collection of unconnected parts.

We were both pretty waterlogged after this particular test and went thankfully over to the pub where the branch was at that time holding its 'dry' meetings. I can remember sitting in an upstairs room, peering with blood-shot eyes (from the chlorine in the baths water!) at what appeared to be some sort of meeting. It soon became clear that this was the Annual General Meeting of the branch. Before I could really do anything about it – or clear the water from my brain – I was elected Secretary. It seemed useless – though I did – to protest that I knew nothing about being a secretary of a diving club for the whole *coup* had the appearance of being carefully worked out beforehand.

'A new outlook, that's what we need,' said the retiring Secretary happily as he passed over his files. Out of four major posts only the vital job of Diving Officer was left in experienced hands!

But it didn't work out too badly. Once we got the hang of things, we really rather looked forward to committee meetings with their attendant supplies of drink. The only drawback was that there appeared to be no hospitality fund for the committee and we had to buy our own.

What we lacked in experience I think it is fair to say we made up in enthusiasm. So perhaps the older hands in the branch were not so daft after all. And I rather looked forward to the moment after several years, of pulling the same trick on some new members that the A.G.M. had pulled on me.

Diving seemed everything then – everything that is to fill our free hours. The time of the tests seemed to be almost over and our open water dives were drawing near. This, despite our enthusiasm, seemed a chilling prospect. People kept talking about breaking the ice on Boxing Day for a fun dive. It didn't sound like fun to me.

The prospect of doing our first 'open water' dives in a lake in early March – after skating round the Boxing Day idea – was also pretty daunting. But this is where 'Mike' Todd turned up trumps.

For some time he had been mumbling away about the dry suits that the club senior divers proudly owned as being obsolete. The new thing, he said, after reading American diving magazines, was the wet suit. It let the water in on purpose. It sounded jolly cold to me, but Mike seemed so full of enthusiasm that I agreed to join a few others in subscribing towards the purchase of some neoprene. Once this was bought, Malcolm Todd was confident that he could produce a 'wet suit' that would keep us warm even if we had to float among icebergs.

Any diver or water-skier nowadays will laugh at the way all of us, except Mike, doubted the 'wet suit'. But you have got to remember that in those days you would find it very difficult to buy a wet suit. One or two manufacturers were toying with the idea, but to the best of our knowledge there was only one commercially made wet suit available in Britain. That was made in France and imported, but all we could find for sale were the naval frogman style of dry suit. True you could wear long underwear and sweaters underneath this, but if the thin rubber was torn by a fingernail or underwater sharp edge you were not only cold, but sinking fast.

Still Mike was making the wet suits and he said it would be all right. So we went along one evening to his Orpington home and were issued with forms listing masses of measurements that were needed. Jean, his wife, was most insistent about the right way to measure – the tape measure must not be too tight, but not too loose.

So we did our best with the help of wives or girlfriends and handed the forms back at the next training night at Downham Baths. The day of the open water dive was rushing upon us and the prospect of an extremely chilly dip was very much in the forefront of my mind. My confidence in the new wet suit was not helped by the scorn poured upon the idea by our instructor, Ken Wise, who described the lake's cold waters with great glee. He, he assured us, would be as warm as toast in his well-tried ex-Navy dry suit.

The suits, as a result of Mike spending every evening glueing pieces of neoprene together, were ready in time. They were made of quarter-inch neoprene and though smooth-faced on inside and out needed copious quantities of French chalk applied to both suit and body to get them on.

Mine was certainly warm enough when I tried it on at home, but the principle of the thing still sounded chilly to me.

All wet suits, even the modern ones nicely lined with nylon to slip on easily without French chalk, work on the same principle. They are a close fit, but not so close that water cannot get in. What happens is that water does get in and forms a layer all over the body inside the suit. But once the water is in, no more can enter. And your body heats up the thin layer of water and, hey presto, you are swimming around in your own warm bath.

It works, but we were not to know that then. So it was with some trepidation that we assembled at Laughing Water, the lake and restaurant on the A.2. near Gravesend.

Ken Wise was still laughing when we emerged from the changing rooms, our faces and hair white from the French chalk we had splattered on the inside of the jacket. 'You'll have whiter faces when you've been in that water,' he said, 'it's freezing!'

Some other divers from another branch looked at us curiously as we passed – they had bagged the best place to get into the water (a wooden landing stage) – for each one was in a dry suit.

I tried the water with my hand when we came to our muddy entrance point. Ken Wise was right – the water was freezing. Still there was no going back now. We pulled on our neoprene hoods, put washing-up gloves on our hands, heaved on the aqualungs and weightbelts. In my case – neoprene is extremely buoyant – that meant – 24 lbs of lead.

Then we stood and listened to Ken Wise's instructions – this after all was not just a test of the Todd wet suit, but also part of our training.

All too soon came the time to enter the water. I waded in slowly and then decided to plunge in the rest of the way and get the shock over quickly. But there was no shock.

True for a moment or two as some water made its way in there was a cringing of flesh, but within seconds I was underwater. And warm! The suit worked. I can remember the rest of that dive with some pleasure. The visibility was only about 8 feet and there was just mud and weed to be seen on the soft bed of the lake – it was so soft with the accumulated ooze of years that you could shove your hand in up to the armpit and still feel no solid bottom – but I was warm.

The only part of me that did get cold was the exposed area of face – around the mouth and lips – that was not covered either by face mask or hood. And even that didn't seem too bad. Laughing Water is spring-fed and the water that seeped in past the aqualung mouthpiece was icy.

The training took about 20 minutes and we each in turn had to do all sorts of manoeuvres, including diving without the lung to the bottom of the lake, where Ken Wise sat on the wreckage of an old rowing boat checking to see that we did not cheat.

There are fish in Laughing Water – and there used to be one big old pike – but we didn't see them on that day though during later dives there I found the sight of young perch among the reeds in sunlit water quite beautiful.

That day it was muddy and dirty and the outside temperature was brisk. I can remember floating on my back when the training was over and waving to Penny and the children, who were all wrapped up in scarves and coats and winter woollies. In fact the coldest part of the whole day was changing out of the suits.

And we had at least one good laugh to cheer us up. We the beginners were nice and warm and comfortable in the water, but before we had finished the veteran, Ken Wise, was shivering and shaking like a leaf. In fact I think I'm right in saying that he put in an order for a Todd Wet Suit before the day was over! Even though we laughed about it, it would not do to think that we were ungrateful for all the time he put into teaching us the art of underwater swimming. He like all the British Sub-Aqua Club instructors gave his time to new members without any idea of financial reward. That was, and is the strength of the Club.

More dives in Laughing Water followed and then Malcolm Todd and I did our first sea dive. Thinking about it now, it was laughable. We strode down the beach at Bognor, Sussex, and waded, then swam out to the reef just off the shore. We saw little – one or two small fish – and the visibility was no more than a foot or two. It was all rather exhausting and a complete waste of time, but we put it down to experience.

I must say that I was unimpressed with that and no more impressed with a visit to Durdle Door. Though it is justly popular as a Dorset diving spot, everything went wrong on that week-end.

It poured with rain – and I mean poured. We staggered down to the sea to meet appalling visibility underwater and appalling conditions above on our return to the surface. Someone held the wrong end of their weightbelt as they were getting into the branch's rubber dinghy – a war-surplus eight-man circular survival raft – and I was dive-bombed with weights as I rose up to follow him.

If this was British diving, I felt it could well do without me.

And left on an early holiday back to Spanish sunshine and clear Mediterranean seas.

What I didn't know was that I was about to come close to dying in those same clear seas – and to find that after one particular dive I was to have a new regular diving companion called Fear.

Chapter
Five

The entry in my diving log-book doesn't look much different from any of the others of the time. Only I know that it is. It is, in fact, a very special entry despite its lack of distinguishing marks. It reads: Site of dive: Sant Elmo. Equipment used: Mistral single. Siebe mid-season. 14 lb. Maximum depth: 115 feet. Duration: 30 minutes. Dive details: Visibility 100 plus. Rock, weed. Purpose and results: Cave exploration. Octopus.

Which being translated means that we dived at Sant Elmo. I was using a single 50 cubic foot cylinder and a Mistral twin hose (one for intake; one for exhaust) with a demand valve attached to it. The suit as noted was a Siebe Gorman mid-season that I had borrowed from Pat Harrison. It was an early version of the modern wet suit (I had left my new quarter-inch Todd suit behind as too warm for Mediterranean waters) and was made of foam-rubber. It had short sleeves and was rather like a sports shirt except that the suit top – and it was only a top – fastened through the crutch. It was a sort of faded yellow and I hoped that at the depth I was intending to go it would provide me with the same sort of warmth that my own wet suit had given me in icy lakes back in England. The '14 lb.' note was to record the amount of lead that I had on my weight belt.

The dive that followed was to change the whole of my underwater life for me for some time and even now it is quite clear in my memory. So I don't think I can improve on the report I wrote of that dive in the London *Evening News* on June 17th, 1967. I wrote it as part of a series of true stories we were running in the paper – and also because I think I hoped by writing it all down that I would lay a ghost that had haunted me for many years.

So here, by permission of the Editor of the *Evening News,* is the way I told it then :

ME AND MY GUN. Early days in the South of France. The shoreline stretching round to St Tropez in the background. (*See* Chapter One)

Raymond Bethoux after a spearfishing trip just off shore of Ste. Maxime. The headless moray eel can be seen on the fish-ring on the left with Andre Fauqueux examining it. (*See* Chapter One)

First visit to Spain. *Left to right:* John Messent, the author, Julian Jubert, who looked after the boat while we dived, and Francisco Castello, whose boat the *Santa Maria del Buen Ayre* is in the background. (*See* Chapter Two)

The shark which frightened the life out of me – here it is after the Sicilian tunnymen had hauled it out of the trap. (*See* Chapter Three)

The first wet suits at Laughing Water. The man in the dry suit on the left is our instructor Ken Wise. Then, *left to right*, the author, Derek Pettitt, Malcolm Todd, who could afford to smile now that the suits he made had passed the cold water test, and Ron Bowler. All members of Bromley Branch of the B.S.A.C. (*See* Chapter Four)

'The bay I hate is no distance from the harbour of San Feliu de Guixols on Spain's Costa Brava.

The rocks slope down into deep water so the sea is blue. The cliffs are a reddish-brown. Grey-trunked, green-topped pine trees cling to the sides of the cliffs in impossible places.

To most people it is a beautiful place. They look down on it from the top and say so. 'What a lovely place for a swim!' they say. But they can swim there. I'd rather not. When I look at that little bay, I shiver despite the heat. You see, I nearly died there – over one hundred feet down beneath that inviting blue surface.

After going through a proper course of aqualung training in this country, I had enjoyed many dives in the waters of the Costa Brava. And like the rest of a crowd who had done their training about the same time, I felt a pretty old hand at the skin-diving game.

We laughed at sentences like: 'There are good divers, bad divers and old divers, but there are no bad old divers.' We were patronising to beginners. We said: 'Never done the ton, old man? ... It's a bit of a bore really – not much to see once you get over a hundred feet, you know.'

In short we were very big-headed. But what was much more dangerous, we were over-confident about our abilities.

It was over-confidence that nearly killed me.

I was on holiday in San Feliu when I met a man who was looking for someone to dive with during his stay.

He was in raptures about a cave he had discovered off the headland of this little bay. This, he said, I had to see ...

We went in off the rocks as far out along the headland as it was possible to go. It was a perfect day on land, and underwater it was beautiful too. Beam of sunlight slanted down through the blue. Every now and then they flickered as a ripple broke the calm of the surface. I slid happily down the lines of warm light. Two sars scurried away at our approach, their thick triangular bodies being driven hard by black-banded tails.

Gradually as we went down the quality of the light changed. Only the big rocks now showed black against the prevailing chilly grey. We were in the hundred foot plus range. A check glance at the depth gauge – a hundred and fifteen feet. Pressure gauge – a hundred atmospheres. Plenty of air in the bottles on our backs.

My new friend swam quickly to the left now. I followed more slowly and lost him in the mist at the edge of vision. But he had not gone far. Suddenly there he was in front and below me.

He appeared to be facing a blank wall of black rock and was looking up at me. I sank down curious to know what had stopped his headlong dash. Unconsciously I had still been hurrying and the rest was welcome. But when I got to him I had a shock. He pointed downward at the rock and beckoned me closer.

When I was right beside him I saw the cave. Cave! It was more like a shallow tunnel leading into the rock. The height of the entrance I estimated at about three feet from top to bottom.

He motioned me on and slid into the entrance himself. I suppose I should have quit then and risked being called chicken but as I slid down to seabed level I could see that the cave was indeed a tunnel.

A narrow tunnel, true, with just about enough room for two divers side by side. It was dark, but a glow of light at the far end seemed only about twenty-five feet away.

My companion switched on the diving torch he carried and the thin beam lit up a marvellous collection of growths glowing red and brilliant on the roof of the cave.

I suddenly felt a pressing need to stay close to a human being and so I spurted into the tunnel, finning so that I was side by side with the torch. Within seconds I felt and heard my bottle scraping the roof above me. Perhaps I had instinctively risen once inside the cave, perhaps the roof sloped downward.

I looked at the floor beneath my eyes and it seemed composed of rounded pebbles all more or less the same size, brown and covered with some furry deposit.

And then to my horror I realised that I was feeling sick and giddy. Oh, no! said my brain silently, I'm not going to die down here. Not here. Not in a miserable cave. Not in all this grey mist. Not here.

I looked up and in my swirling vision I could see the bubbles of expired air from the demand valves on our backs clinging like upside-down grey jellies to the roof of solid rock above me.

I wanted above all to get to the end. I kicked hard and within seconds – though it seemed longer – was out into the grey light at the open end.

Once outside I rose instinctively about ten feet. Every story I had ever read and disregarded about the dangers of being sick into your breathing tubes at depth leapt into my mind. Then I had thought this is only for fools who dive immediately after drinks or a huge meal.

Yet here was I just about to die the same way with only a cup of coffee and a buttered roll with thin, sticky Spanish marmalade inside me.

I imagined the blocking of the air tubes. The scene around me spun. I took great deep drags on my mouthpiece and felt only surprise when air rushed into my lungs and my head cleared.

My companion tapped my arm and pointed downward to a rock nearby and I realised with some shock, though my head and stomach were settling fast, that I was looking into two large eyes. Eyes that I had swum inches over in my rush for the light.

There on the rock that partially blocked the exit to the tunnel cave was the largest octopus that I have ever seen. His body looked three feet across, his tentacles much longer.

All I wanted to do now was to go up, but my companion raised his torch as though to hit the octopus. I could see it react. First the rear tentacles took a tighter grip on the rock, writhing and twisting underneath it for better holds. Then the tentacles nearer to the front tensed. And lifted in the water – ready.

The last thing I wanted at that moment was a game with an octopus. I signalled frantically to my companion that I wanted to go up. He acknowledged with a nod and gave the octopus what I presume was meant to be a friendly tap on the head with his waterproof torch. One tentacle immediately flicked up, whip-like, and grabbed the torch.

It was only the tip of the tentacle that made contact with the torch, but even so it took a good pull to break the grip. My companion seemed to be laughing. I had had enough. If that octopus had grabbed at me as I flicked over the top of him in my panic coming out of the cave, I don't know that I could have been responsible for my nerves.

I signalled up, and up we went. It seemed to take years for the mirror of the surface to appear shining above me. More time to break through into the sun and air of that bay.

At that moment it was beautiful. Now I hate it. Perhaps I shouldn't. After all, I did learn a lesson. The reason that I had felt sick and nearly passed out down there was simply that I had held my breath. Because I was frightened. Not a great big experienced diver at all really. Just a frightened one, whose panic could have killed him.

And that is what that bay reminds me of each time I see it. And why it gives me the shivers.'

It continued to give me the shivers for some time to come. I don't think that I really like that bay even now.

But what I wasn't able to tell in that report was the effect that dive had on the future of my diving. I was considerably more shaken than even that description conveys. I felt sick with fear at the thought of diving – any kind of diving, not just deep.

I knew that my nerve had gone very quickly. And I hoped that it would come back just as quickly. But I knew in my heart that it wouldn't. Not that I didn't try it out. That very evening I went for a shallow dive – no more than 35 feet – off the rocks at the right hand side of Conca Beach. But it wasn't any good. As soon as I was underwater I felt a shortness of breath, unease, unhappiness and general alarm. I tried taking some pictures with the Box Brownie in its case, but even this did not distract me from the fact that there seemed a great deal of water over my head and all I really wanted to do was to get out of the water.

Now no one could call Conca an unfriendly place. Pine trees crowd down to the beach and even in the early evening it was full of tourist swimmers. Conca is not very far from San Feliu and, if you walk there, your route takes you through the 'millionaires estate' of S'Agaro. It is only recently that armed guards stop cars with no business going through and that the Hotel Gavina there has obtained the final accolade of the residence of a British Foreign Secretary on holiday. But it is still a lovely place. Lovely enough for the film moguls to take all their exterior shots for 'Sinbad the Sailor' on the beach – though they had to build a few fake boulders and plaster of paris castles for their romance.

It is on Conca beach, too, that I have seen the way that fish adapt to the tourist invasion. It is extraordinary to put on a mask and watch the usually shy sars move in and out of the feet of the unwitting bathers snapping up the delicacies that foreign feet have aroused from the sand.

And those who say that it is nonsense to report that fish are aware of hostile shapes such as that of a speargun should hang there in the shallow water with a mask and watch what happens when a tourist injects a gun into the scene. The fish, which only a few moments before were thick among, but not touching, the feet of the bathers are, almost the moment that the gun is visible, gone.

Penny I know was aware of my fear before I mentioned it. It seemed a shameful thing to confess to her, but once I had done so I felt a sense of relief. At least I didn't have to keep up the pretence with her.

It took more self-argument to confess my fear to others, but I knew it had to be done and so I deliberately sought out Pat Harrison at the time I knew he would be leaving his training area at Port Salvi.

I didn't have long to wait before Pat came toiling up the slope with his own twin set slung on his back. At least it is hardly fair to say that he toiled. He walked remarkably quickly while the three or four trainees that he had with him found the going much harder – and they toiled.

He stopped and we chatted. 'Have you got a moment, Pat?' I asked him quietly and we stopped and let the others go on. And then I told him what had happened – and said point blank that I was frightened of diving.

His reaction was swift. 'Have you got your gear with you? There's only one cure . . . and that's to go back in now.' I was touched by his kindness. He must have had enough of diving for one day but he was prepared to go all the way back down the rocks and take me in at that very moment.

I thanked him, but suggested that we should dive the next

day. He seemed to think that any time lost was a mistake, but we finally agreed to meet and dive the next morning. I must say I was comforted by his concern and told myself that everything would be all right now.

But it wasn't. As I put on the diving gear on the rocks next morning the prospect of the dive filled me with dismay. I got cross with a strap that just wouldn't seat properly on my shoulders and knew that my irritation was only a sign of nerves. And those same nerves were not helped by the knowledge that the cure, if this was to be a cure, would not come in just a few feet of sunlit water. If I was going to get over my fear we were going to have to go deep.

And deep we went. At about 80 feet I felt my heart beating in my ears and equalising the pressure only stopped the loud thumping and reduced it to a quieter tone. I began to breathe faster and remembered all my training warned against breathing so fast that you 'beat the lung' – the time lag in the mechanism of the demand valve will prevent continuous heavy panting.

I slowed my fin action and tried to relax. Pat Harrison noted my slowed pace and moved in protectively. I let myself drift and after a few seconds regained control of myself. Pat gave me the divers' O.K. signal with his forefinger and thumb looped together. It was a question and I answered O.K. in the same way. And we went on down.

Soon our descent levelled out and we were gliding over rippled sand. I didn't look at my depth gauge. If the gauge had shown me over the 100 foot mark, I felt that it would only upset me.

But Pat Harrison was magnificent. We stopped there and he lay on his back on the sand, folded his arms, and pretended to go to sleep. Then he opened his eyes and gave me one enormous wink. The point of this clowning was obvious, but even so I began to feel better. It couldn't be all that bad if a man could fool about down here.

Then he showed me his depth gauge. The pointer was well over the 30 metre mark (100 feet plus). I felt a new sense of achievement. Not a bad depth for a coward. The whole set up struck me as being amusing and eerie at the same time. My demand valve developed a sort of singing squeak – some do at depth; there is nothing wrong with them they just do it – and in the semi-luminous haze over the sand it seemed to echo weirdly.

After a few moments Pat signalled that we should start back. I felt some relief at this, so I was obviously not a great big brave diver yet. Instead of going back the way we had come, we moved up to the right and at about 60 feet paused over the green banks of eel grass.

Over the tips of the weed there were swarms of little black and violet fishes – those same sea flies that I had watched so often before. But these were really tiny and though perfect miniatures of their parents were difficult to watch closely unless you put your face mask right down on to them.

It was while doing this that my heart gave a thump of surprise. Standing out of the growth among the clump roots of the weed was something that was immediately recognisable as a pottery handle. I grabbed at it and it came free in my hand. I thought for a moment that I had found a Roman amphora, but on scrabbling round among the weed I found other bits of pottery that made it quite clear that what I was holding was much more modern. It was a shattered wine jar of some sort, but much smaller than the usual amphora. Some people I showed the pieces to later thought it was probably 17th or 18th century – the growth on it was extensive so it had certainly been in the sea for many, many years.

I waved the handle and hooted at Pat Harrison who was only a few yards away. He sped towards me at full fin power. I think that, for a moment, he thought I was in trouble.

Then we both searched for more pieces. But if they were there we couldn't find them. And then it was time to go up. As we did so I realised the most extraordinary thing. I had forgotten all about being frightened. From the moment I had found the pottery all fear had gone from my mind. Occupational therapy.

As we broke surface, Pat pushed up his mask, spat out his mouthpiece and said: 'All right?' 'All right,' I said, 'and thank you!' 'Any time,' he said grinning back. And then we swam towards the rocks in the sunshine.

I felt good as I towelled myself off, but I wasn't fool enough to think that I was completely cured. Pat Harrison had repaired my nerves, but fear was to stay with me for a long, long time yet. And I don't suppose I shall ever forget that cave.

Oddly enough that cave was visited again by divers some years later and one of them J. David George of Chelsea Branch, B.S.A.C., wrote about it. His article on a diving holiday in San Feliu de Guixols appeared in the February 1969 issue of *Watersports and Sub-Aqua World*. The relevant part of it is reproduced here by kind permission of the Editor, Leo Zanelli.

Mr George wrote: 'Our attention had been drawn during the holiday to a short article written some time ago by Kendall McDonald for a national newspaper in which he describes his unfortunate experiences in a cave over 100 feet down off the headland near Port Salvi. Joan Harrison believed that she knew the cave to which he referred and gave us instructions on how to locate it in order that we could make it the objective of our final holiday dive.

We snorkelled round the headland to the right of the bay until we found a rocky pinnacle 4–5 feet below the surface and some 20 yards offshore, this being the first marker on our dive. As we rested on the pinnacle shoals of fish swam round our feet, their bodies flashing silver in the dancing light.

Within a few minutes our breathing slowed to normal after our longish snorkel swim and so we sank below the surface and started to descend a gully leading in an offshore direction from the pinnacle. At 60 feet the gully opened out into a small sandy clearing before plunging down again to the sandy seabed at about 95 feet. The cave we had been assured was somewhere near the opening of the gully on to the sand.

We decided to cast off to the right along the rocks in the hope of finding the entrance. Alas! after swimming about 40 yards there was still no sign of the cave, so we decided to retrace our path back to the exit of the gully. However, every gully looks very much like the next underwater and we never really located the point from which we started the search.

I would estimate that we had swum 50 yards back (i.e. 10 yards to the left of the gully) before sighting a black gash in the rock where it met the sand. Probably at one time the entrance had been higher, but has gradually become silted with sand.

Now the entrance was about 10 feet wide and rose from

about six inches on the left to a height of three feet on the right. Switching on our torches we flattened ourselves on the bottom and finned cautiously in with the needles of our depth gauges hovering on the 100 foot mark. This certainly wasn't the place for someone with claustrophobic tendencies, although once inside the entrance the height of the cave increased to about six feet.

Once our eyes were accustomed to the gloom we could see a faint glimmer of light about 30 feet away indicating an exit from the tunnel. Slowly moving forward we noted that the roof and walls of the cave were covered with sponges of many hues interspersed with hundreds of bright yellow anemones.

Here and there were small sprigs of the precious red coral. This coral which shuns strong illumination fetches a high price and consequently tempts many commercial aqualung divers in the Mediterranean to risk their lives at great depths collecting it.

Our exhaust bubbles instead of rising in a majestic silver trail above us as they do in open water were rolling around on the roof of the cave like great amoeboid masses ever increasing in size as the bubbles coalesced together. The exit from the cave proved to be a roughly circular opening about three feet in diameter in the roof. Exiting from the cave into the seemingly brilliant light at 90 feet we began our slow ascent to the surface well pleased with our last dive.'

Did I suffer from claustrophobic tendencies on my dive in that cave? I don't know. But I do know that I missed seeing that coral. All I wanted to do was to get out and up!

Chapter

Six

Though Pat Harrison had given me back some of my nerve, I was still pretty shattered. The best thing that could have happened after that was for me to have taken my diving very easily and so gently eased myself back into full confidence.

A dive the very next day told me that fear was not completely banished. I plunged down, side by side with Penny, happily enough until we reached about 80 feet, but then suddenly felt slightly giddy. I checked and Penny glided past me down to the flat sand of the seabed. I hooted at her desperately through my mouthpiece to come back, but she didn't hear.

I didn't want to go any further down – in fact I would have been much happier higher up. The feeling eased a little, but I still watched her carefully as she moved some 15 feet below me, gliding with arms outspread like an aeroplane and obviously enjoying every minute. And I still wanted to go up. I cursed making the words vibrate my mouthpiece – 'for God's sake come back'. I beckoned and she rose to my level. I pointed to my ears and shook my head, then wobbled my hand from side to side to indicate that I wasn't feeling so good. She looked at me curiously, eyes wide through the glass of her mask.

We rose into the sunlight and every foot we went up made me happier. We swanned around at about 45 feet for a time and then, because there was nothing new to see, ended the dive and broke out into the hot sunshine and shimmering rocks of the bay.

'I didn't feel well down there – sort of giddy,' I said, not even admitting to myself that what I really thought I had experienced was fear. Penny didn't say very much and I felt I had let her down. The onset of giddiness worried me – not because I didn't really know that I was frightened – but because I began to wonder if the giddiness brought on the fear. Or did the fear bring on the giddiness?

The odd thing about all this was that I never thought for a moment of giving up diving. I thought I was going through a temporary phase, the sort of thing that was bound to follow a bad fright. All I really needed I told myself was a few quiet dives in reasonably shallow water and I should soon be quite all right again.

I was probably right in this diagnosis, but it was not to be. That very evening before dinner I wandered around the shops of San Feliu. And walked right into it.

It took the form of a plump Spaniard called Fernando. And it also involved three British Sub-Aqua Club divers on holiday in San Feliu.

Fernando was going on a dive the very next day. It was, to the best of my recollection a Saturday night when we talked, so the dive was scheduled for Sunday. And Fernando was expansive to the extent of being able to include some other divers in on the trip. Actually I'm pretty certain that the inclusion of other divers would allow the costs to come down to the sort of figure that Fernando thought reasonable for his pocket.

Fernando started to expand to the three British divers and myself, in a mixture of Spanish, Catalan, French and English on the beauties of diving on the Costa Brava. Had we seen this? Or that? Had we dived through the famous tunnel in the Medas Islands up near Rosas? We had not.

Now there is nothing like local knowledge abroad – and this applies more to diving than anything else. You can spend days diving around a certain spot and only find out on your return that you missed the most famous dive of all and you grit your teeth with fury when reading about it in a diving magazine at home.

I think all the British divers could have resisted Fernando's diving baits until he revealed that the very next day he was going to dive for coral. And if we wanted to come along we would be very welcome.

The three others leapt at the chance. My hesitation was only momentary. A little warning voice inside me said that coral was only to be found at great depths and made it quite clear that great depths were not for me at that particular time. I knew it, but found myself agreeing to join the

75

party. We would meet outside a local diving shop at 8 a.m. and go to the boat in the harbour immediately we were all together.

Fernando then gave us a short lecture on the difficulty of collecting the red precious coral and produced a number of coral hammers – they looked just like a geologist's hammer to me – which were for sale at extremely reasonable prices. He sold a hammer or two. I refrained. I knew that I was going to be lucky to reach coral depth anyway – particularly as Fernando kept on about it being at a depth in excess of 'trenta metros', which meant over 100 feet . . .

Penny was still in bed when I left the next morning. 'Don't go down if you don't want to. It doesn't matter,' she said. I knew then that she knew I was dreading it.

The four British divers were on time at the rendezvous so was a Belgian, but there was no sign of Fernando. When he finally turned up, we had discussed all the *mañana* habits of the Spanish and were considering Fernando in particular. But he had arrived and for that we supposed we could count our blessings.

The gear was soon heaved into our cars and the little convoy set off through the sleeping Ramblas of the town and out along the long arm of the harbour. San Feliu slept in the early sun. It's a good time if you feel fit – the sun has not had long enough to get to full heat and you feel sort of Commando-like as you move through the deserted streets. The sun is welcoming, but not painful as it is at full day and there is a coolness about that can come at no other time. It's clean too somehow and the tyres of the car thwack on the road and almost echo in the empty air. But the prevailing impression is of cleaness and coolness – and the town seems to be resting.

The sight of the boat surprised me. We pulled up close to the wall of the harbour arm and looked down a flight of steps to the oily calm of the protected water. Fernando engaged in some bandinage with the two man crew and the sun bounced off the oil slicks into our eyes. The boat was much bigger than I had expected. I guessed its length at about 24 feet. Rather like a Thames barge with a thin drain-pipe smoke stake sticking out a short way from the stern.

It wasn't however what you would call a super boat. Not

new or anything like that. Battered, old and sun-beaten are words that you could fairly apply.

We heaved the gear down the steps and soon cleared the harbour arm. There wasn't much difference between the sea outside and the oily calm inside the harbour. Just a very slight chop appeared once we rounded the great stone blocks on which the harbour wall had been built.

The sun was warm, but not hot and we lolled about and chatted. The sunlight bouncing off the water made us sleepy and the steady thump-thump of the engine added to our doziness.

The coast of Spain from the sea on a Sunday morning could be a look at days gone by. Beaches are deserted. Even the hardy British tourist doesn't venture on them at that time. I have done the trip up and down the Costa Brava many times since and I never cease to be impressed by the early morning coastline so devoid of people, and from the superior vantage point of a boat, so much better for it.

The sun was now hitting the water at an angle which made the glare painful if you tried to look into it even with sunglasses. The diving gear itself made poor pillows, but the collection of kitbags into which we had stuffed the diving extras were soft enough to lounge against. I listened drowsily to Fernando expounding on the art of collecting coral. One should never grab at it, he said, or the stem would break off in your hand leaving only a few shattered fragments of the branches. The ideal method of collecting was to chip the base away from the rock itself – and if you were careful you should have in your hands not only a fine branch of coral, but also all of the thick stem itself. Coral grew downwards from the overhangs or in caves and was only found on the east side of the islands.

The islands? This was the first time that I became fully aware that we were heading for real islands off the coast of the Costa Brava. Not that it mattered very much. If the sea remained this calm even a pedalo could have been bicycled all the way to North Africa.

My doze was shattered violently by yells from the boat's Spanish skipper. I sat up and was amazed to see that the engine hatch was on fire. But it wasn't serious and a bucket of blue from over the side soon put paid to what small flames there were. The engine cover had been resting against the 'smoke stack' which' which by now was red-hot. The captain and the engineer exchanged some Catalan that needed no interpreter to be translated into recriminations. Just to make sure the engine hatch was dipped in the sea and the charred edges around the portion which fitted close to the exhaust were carefully soaked.

Apart from that the voyage was uneventful. After about an hour and a half, Fernando pointed : 'Las Formigas'. And there were our islands. Not that you could call them luxuriant oases in the blue Mediterranean. Just a cluster of pale-orange rocks without the slightest suspicion of vegetation on them.

The little group justified the description of islands though. The largest was about 30 feet above sea level at its highest point and from a distance showed all the signs of having deep water around it. If that sounds a rather sweeping statement – how can anyone tell the depth of water around a rock from a distance? – all sailors will know that the look of the water will tell you something about the depth, but more important the lie of the land will tell you much more about the water that runs up to it.

For example, if you see a flat coastline gently shelving down to the sea, you can be pretty sure that the land under the sea will continue the same gentle slope. If, however, the land falls steeply into the sea, then it will continue in the same fall underwater. In fact any diver will confirm this. Sheer cliffs mean sheer cliffs underwater. Gentle sloping sands mean gentle sloping sands underwater. Of course these are generalisations and it may well be that a geological fault can upset these interpretations. But that is more likely to be the exception than the rule.

It was the same with the Formigas Islands. The main island's small peak fell straight into the sea promising deep water on the eastern side. The South-West – from which we were approaching – was different. Here small outcrops of rock away from the main island promised shallower depths. In my heart I rejoiced in this. If all else failed I could always work through the group and have a pleasant dive in shallower water. But for the time being I stiffened my mind to going down into the really deep water for some coral. All I was doing mentally was of course, preparing my escape route if my nerves failed to stand up to the depth.

Fernando was climbing into a full suit – a full dry suit of the old-fashioned kind – even before we were close to the rocks which now looked like the lava overflow from some extinct volcano. Everyone else started preparing their equipment. They all seemed excited and happy at the prospect of diving. I followed suit more slowly. I felt alone in my fear of deep water. Everyone else was looking forward to it – why couldn't I?

We moved in close to the island now and to all of our surprise – all that is except Fernando – the captain showed no sign of stopping his engine to let us get off. He gesticulated to us to jump. Fernando clutched his mask tight to his face and leapt out into the wake.

For a second he bobbed in a cloud of bubbles on the surface and then was gone into the blue. The Belgian whom I suspected was a little less happy than anyone else except me followed him. I must say this surprised me. I don't know if you can say that fear breeds comradeship – certainly wartime experiences suggest it does – but the Belgian had, I felt, a certain rapport with me about the whole dive. With his jump into space over the stern he severed this connection.

The British contingent hesitated. This certainly was not the kind of diving entry they had been used to. No one could understand why it was necessary to do this sort of parachutist entry into the water when all the captain had to do was to stop his engines and let us all go into the water in a decent civilised manner.

Our problem was solved when the Belgian surfaced in our wake obviously in trouble. He waved frantically in the water for assistance and seemed to be drowning. We yelled at the captain. He cursed and pushed the boat's big tiller across to swing in a circle and head back the way we had come.

At the end of the circuit as he still showed no sign of stopping the engines two more of us leapt out over the foaming wake. When the cloud of entry bubbles cleared it was a vast relief to see the big propeller spinning underwater – away from us.

The Belgian was in trouble. Choking and gasping for air he indicated between gulps that the demand valve of his aqualung had failed. He clutched at one of the British divers and started to drag him under. Coolly the Briton inflated his life-jacket and let him hang on. With life-jacket inflated there was little that the Belgian could do about drowning either himself or his rescuer. I must say that at this moment the whole dive seemed to me to be not worth it. I would happily have climbed back aboard and paid the captain for his trouble.

Round came the boat again. To my relief this time it paused nearby. The prop. still turned slowly, but the drive was obviously disconnected. We pushed the Belgian aboard and no sooner had his fins disappeared over the gunwhale than the engine started again and the two remaining B.S.A.C. divers leapt out over the wake to join us.

The whole thing seemed to be happening in a dream. The captain's behaviour I found so extraordinary that there must be some logical explanation if only I had time to think about it. But there we were, a cluster of divers on the surface with the Formigas main island towering over us and the diving boat heading purposefully away as though to abandon us for ever.

So I had little time to think about it. Suddenly Fernando was below and fins were turning up to the sky. Regardless of the odd behaviour of the diving boat's captain, the dive for coral was obviously beginning.

Loneliness set in immediately. The sun was shadowed by the rocks and gloom seemed only a few feet below as I angled down through the water after the bubbles of the lead divers. It wasn't all that much better when we came out of the shadow into sunlight. the water below looked grey-green then black and there was not the slightest sign of any bottom. I had some trouble clearing my ears, which put me even further behind. One of the British divers looked back, saw me trailing and started back. I pointed to my ears and signalled him to go on. Soon the only sign of life below me was a champagne white fizz coming from far below as those without fear breathed their way down to the coral.

I suppose that having chosen to be alone like that I should

have felt more frightened, but I didn't. I wasn't happy, but I wasn't so terrified either. I hummed to myself into my mouth-piece. It wasn't too bad. I followed the bubbles – so tiny that they must have been very deep below me – along the sides of a sheer rock. I looked at my depth gauge – 70 feet – then at my contents gauge. I had plenty of air. I made a very firm resolve to start ascending before the needle moved into the red. I would start coming up as soon as I had only 30 atmosphere left. That is what I had been taught; that is what I definitely intended to do.

The sheer wall of dark rock gave way to an overhang. At first I thought it was a cave, but it didn't go back very far. I hung there for a moment or two, trying to decide what to do. I was just on the point of turning back and heading for the shallower section of the islands that I had spotted on the approach run when something feathery and white almost in front of my nose caught my eye. I moved back to get the growth in focus. And realised with an upwelling of heart that I was looking straight at a piece of coral. It didn't look anything like the pictures that you see in underwater books, where flash bulbs have been used to bring out the red.

My first inclination was to snatch at it. My hand was almost on when I remembered Fernando's words Snatch and the coral shatters. My hand had however moved close enough to frightened the coral polyps. The white disappeared and near my hand was just a rose-grey twig. If the white polyps had not been out I would never have recognised it as coral.

Now I drew my knife from its leg sheath and carefully prised away at the twig's base. It dropped free – into my hand – and I almost lost it. Now I understood Fernando's insistence on a net in which to catch coral. It had seemed just more clutter to carry at the time.

Even underwater the twig felt fragile and I held it gently by the stem as I went up towards the sunlight. My coral diving was over – and I felt it just too good to be true that I would actually have a piece of coral to show for it. But suddenly a new doubt assailed me. Was it really coral? Had I fallen for the false coral that Fernando had mentioned so casually on the boat?

Any doubt I might have had disappeared as I moved into

shallower water. The twig in my hand started to glow and by the time I could see the surface the whole coral was a glorious fluorescent red.

This burst into crimson glory is the most beautiful thing about bringing either coral or gorgonia to the surface. Some of the gorgonia you find in the Mediterranean – often like coral it favours the eastern side of some deep rock face – looks at depth green with faded yellow tips. Yet as you bring it to the surface the green turns into a riot of reds and the faded yellow burns like bright yellow poster paint in a spotlight.

So often a non-diver sitting in a boat when the divers surface will believe that all those glorious colours are there deep down. The divers will use the fact that a cut bleeds grey or greeny-grey at depth to illustrate the lack of colour far below, but I am not sure that the explanation ever penetrates. The onlooker has that dreamy look about the eyes that reveals only too well that for him or her the undersea world is a riot of reds and yellows and those dreadful divers are only trying to keep the deep sea's secrets to themselves.

So I had my coral – and I still had my nerve. I levelled off at about 20 feet and found, to my surprise, that a strong current ran between the islands from east to west.

I was carried along, not too fast, but enough to let myself drift and take in the underwater scenery. The Formigas under-water are a splendid sight. Beneath me now was a jumbled boulder seabed – to my right it tumbled away to the depths – and the sunlight made pretty patterns on the rocks.

I didn't try to fight the current. It was carrying me in the right direction and when I emerged from between the islands I was sure that I would find some handy rock on which to climb. I would then wait to be picked up.

It was all going splendidly. Until I became aware that I was not alone. Travelling at almost the same speed, but deeper and slightly to the front was a big silver fish. At first he struck me as a splendid sight. A bass? No definitely not; the wrong shape. Dentex? No. Grey mullet? No. As I mentally ran back through the pages of my reference books, a picture came into mind. I rejected it. Impossible. But was it? That cold eye fixed on me. The pike-like head. The long body. And with a click of memory I was sure. My companion was a barracuda. I tried to shove the idea away. In the Mediterranean? Impossible.* Even so I was glad when with a slight flick of the tail he was gone and I was alone again. And I made sure that I was alone by twisting round in the water to check in all directions.

The current quickened a little now and swept me between two underwater rock walls and suddenly I was out in the open sea. The Formigas towered up behind me and I began to look for the low rocks I had seen. The trouble was that close to they weren't so low. The happiness of a successful dive began to fade a little. I drifted over the complete skeleton of a wooden boat that had obviously not found the Formigas a friendly place. It looked so intact that I imagined it had been scuttled –the ribs were all intact, but the decking had long since vanished.

I thought about diving down to it, but the problem of making some sort of landfall decided me against it. A shallow reef loomed up and I managed to balance on it with my head out of water. Should I blow my life-jacket? I decided against it. It was difficult enough to stay standing on the rocks leaning into the current without having an inflated life-jacket provide more drag.

So I waited for the boat. And waited and waited. Loneliness began to set in. About 400 yards away a life-jacket inflated and a dark head bobbed in its yellow ring. Any comfort I felt soon disappeared as the yellow ring got smaller and smaller and finally could only be seen if I craned my head round behind me.

Other life-jackets blossomed in the distance and got further and further away like the first. Closer at hand, near one of the main islands of the group, another black-suited figure managed to scramble out of the water and perched on a rock to wait for the boat.

The non-appearance of the boat was now more than mysterious. It was intensely worrying. Surely nothing could have happened to it in such calm waters. I remembered the wreck over which I had just swum and worried even more. Something

* Barracuda do exist in the Mediterranean. Captain Ted Falcon-Barker has photographs of barracuda he speared from a shoal that hovered near an underwater fresh-water spring in the sea off Ibiza.

else was missing from the sunlit scene, but it was some time be-before I could pin down what it was. Then I realised that there was not the slightest sound except for the lapping of the water on the nearby rocks. Why couldn't I hear the reverberating thump of the boat's engines? At first I told myself it was because the boat was behind the islands and all engine noise was being blocked by the rock faces, but as time went on, the silence itself became another worry. The captain had been anxious not to stop his engine before – why wasn't it still running now?

I answered this one with some reflections on the Spanish character that were grossly unfair. I visualised the captain and his engineer fast asleep on the sun-soaked deck of the diving boat. After all it must be getting on towards noon. Didn't all Spaniards nap in the midday sun? And if my theory was right, how were we going to wake them up?

My ponderings on this were interrupted several times when I slipped off the ledge of rock and floundered about trying to get back again. But the final interruption to worry came not from this, but from the stream of angry shouts that came from the solitary diver perched on the rock on the islands. Even as far away as I was I could identify the fury and the language. It was Spanish. That identified the diver on the rock as Fernando.

What he was shouting at suddenly emerged around the corner of the most northerly island of the group. It was the boat at last. But there was something peculiar about its progress. The silence remained unbroken except for Fernando's fury floating across the water to me. The boat was being propelled as fast as such a boat could be propelled – by oars. Oars is the wrong word for those great sweeps and even from my distant point of view it was clear what labour was going into moving the boat at all.

It inched forward closer and closer to Fernando and finally he considered it close enough to deign to come down off his rock and enter the water.

When I saw him move I decided to swim to it too. It was a long swim against the current but I felt it would be better to get to the boat while I could. Heaven knows what might happen to it next. I was also vastly concerned about those tiny yellow dots of divers that I had last seen disappearing into the distance behind me.

Once aboard I cut short the continuing argument between Fernando and the crew to demand a reason for the lack of engine. It took time, but finally I understood. The diesel in the boat depended for ignition on the top of the cylinder being heated with a blowlamp. Fuel for the engine they had in plenty, but paraffin for the blowlamp none. I suddenly realised the reason why the captain had insisted on the paratrooper-style of our entry into the water at the start of the dive. He had known that if once he stopped the engine he would be unlikely to start it.

Was there no paraffin at all? And then came the most amazing disclosure of all. No, they had no paraffin, but a fisherman in a little boat nearby had some. Then why the hell didn't they borrow some from him? That, to them, was simple. The man was a robber. He wanted ten pesetas for a small bottle. It was daylight robbery on the high seas and they weren't going to pay it.

I lost my temper. I rummaged through my diving bag, found a 25-peseta piece and flung it to the fisherman in the little boat which was now alongside. He handed over the paraffin and within a short time we were mobile again.

Fortunately every diver was picked up without trouble, but anyone who believes the Mediterranean is a current-less sea, would have been amazed at the distance we had to travel before all were accounted for and safely on board.

All the British divers had their coral, but Fernando had done best of all. Much of the coral, he told us, would go to the local scientific laboratories for examination – and he generously handed each of us another piece. In return all the British divers admitted that in the art of coral diving Fernando was certainly a master of the craft.

The voyage back to port was uneventful. We had all learned a lot – not the least that only a fool goes diving without a life-jacket. I had learned too that although my nerve was coming back it would be well not to push it too hard for a while. I knew this even more strongly when I joined Penny for a very late lunch in the shaded patio of the Hotel Murla – showed her my coral trophies* – and felt a mad rush of happiness to be back – and alive.

Spanish coral is the precious red coral (Corallium rubrum) and requires skill and patience to polish. In some Spanish jewellers you will see whole 'branches' that have been polished. This is an extremely tricky job as the coral becomes brittle when subjected to the heat generated by the polishing wheel and tends to snap.

The penalties for taking coral without permission are severe and tourist divers should be warned that the least that may happen if they do so, and are caught doing so, is complete confiscation of all diving gear and the boat from which the diving has taken place.

* At the time when I dived for coral it was not expressly forbidden by Spanish law. Now special permission is required to dive for coral and it is rarely granted as it seems clear that most of the coral diving concessions have been sold to professional Italian firms.

Chapter
Seven

Sooner or later every diver wants to see a wreck. Not necessarily a wreck that no one else has found – that is the stuff that divers' dreams are made of – but a wreck of some kind, and the more like a real ship the better.

Unfortunately, underwater wrecks are seldom anything like the wrecks of films and fiction. Most are crumbling old scrapheaps on the seabed, but this will not disappoint the diver to the point where he gives up wreck diving because some wrecks – just a few – are just like the popular idea of a sunken ship.

More ships have sunk around the coasts of Britain than any other country in the world – that's the price of being a trading nation – and out of all those ships some are almost intact in their watery graves.

Most divers know of the good ones. They've been dived over and over again for the thrill of seeing a ship loom up out of the gloom and the excitement of finning through fishes over their decks and holds.

One of the best known is the s.s. *Maine*, a 3,600 ton cargo ship outward bound from London and torpedoed on March 23rd, 1917. Salvers tried to tow her to shore and failed by one mile. She sank, upright, one mile from Bolt Head in Devon.

Now the *Maine* lies on an even keel on the seabed 120 feet down and stands some 50 feet proud of the bottom shingle. The Torbay Branch of the British Sub-Aqua Club have bought her, and they do not mind anyone diving on her, but insist that no one takes souvenirs off her. Incidentally, Branch divers succeeded in raising her bronze propeller in the largest amateur marine salvage operation on record in this country.

The *Maine* is intact except for some of her superstructure – even down to a gun on her poop – but most divers are not fortunate enough to see such a wreck-like wreck on their first wreck dives.

My first wreck, for example, was a rather more modest affair. I don't know now how the diving trip began, but someone knew someone, who knew a fisherman, who knew a fisherman, who knew where there was a wreck. Now it would be a pretty odd fisherman who didn't know where there was a wreck, but this one was different in that he knew exactly where it was (at least he seemed very confident about it) and was prepared to take us out to it.

Not all fishermen like taking divers out. Some, of course, have better things to do – like fishing. Others believe these silly stories about divers robbing lobster pots and don't want their more militant colleagues to see them collaborating with the 'robbers'. And some others find it more financially rewarding to take out parties of sea anglers, who don't have so much gear as divers and so can be packed rod to rod along the boat's sides.

One would have hoped that this 'divers robbing lobster pots myth' would have died by now because it just doesn't make sense. But it still lingers on. Taking lobsters by hand as divers do is difficult enough – the idea is to get your hand round behind and grip the brute's back well away from those nasty nippers. Imagine how difficult it would be if the lobster is in a pot. A lobster when hauled to the surface and tackled in the air is, I can assure you, a very sombulant creature indeed when compared with the same fellow in his own element 40 feet down in the sea. In a pot you'd lose your fingers. So if there was the pot-robbing going on that some fishermen pretend there is, there'd be a lot of fingerless divers around too!

But back to wreck diving. My first wreck was at Dover. In Crab Bay to be precise. And she was a steel sailing ship called the *Preussen*, sunk in November, 1910.

That was all we knew about her at the time. I remember that Reg Dunton and Mike Todd were part of the group of Bromley Branch divers who gathered on the quay at Dover. The weather wasn't too good on that April Sunday, but the sea didn't look too bad outside the harbour mouth.

We anchored right under the towering white cliffs and the boatman said that we were right over the wreck. Two divers probed the bottom in about ten feet of visibility. She wasn't there. As we looked at the boatman with eyes that had no respect in them, the tide sank still more and 30 yards away what was obviously a piece of wreckage broke the surface. 'There she is,' said the boatman triumphantly.

We prepared to dive . . .

The *Preussen* was a giant five-masted sailing ship, the only one of her class built in 1902 and was, at the time of her sinking, the largest sailing ship afloat.

Her length was 407 feet, nine inches. Her beam was 53 feet, seven inches. Her registered tonnage was 4,768 and she was called a steel ship because she was in fact steel-plated.

The *Preussen*'s last voyage was intended to be from Hamburg, her home port, to Valparaiso with general cargo. On November 6th, 1910, she was off Newhaven when she was in collision with the Channel steamer *Brighton* plying between Newhaven and Dieppe as part of the Paris-London service.

The *Brighton* lost her forward funnel, her mainmast and much of her port side was crushed, but the *Preussen* was in a worse state. Her foremast was gone, she had taken heavy damage in the bow section and her 80-foot long bowsprit was bent like a banana. Captain Heinrich Nissen, her Master, would have been all right, for his pumps were holding their own with the leaks, if it had not been for the worsening weather. A gale was coming up and finally the squalls got so strong that towlines to tugs parted and the *Preussen* was driven on to the rocks of Crab Bay.

They tried and tried to get her off, but it was no use – the hull was pierced in two places and she was doomed. And salvage work began on her cargo as soon as the weather eased.

So we dived fifty years later. The wreck lies the same way as the ship struck, broadside on to the cliff. And by the time it came to my turn to dive, the tide had started to run and visibility was down to eight feet.

Low visibility diving is quite normal for British divers. And sites such as this one close into the shore suffer from poorer visibility than the deeper waters farther out to sea. Sometimes, of course, it gets so bad that you are pushing through a brown fog with the added frustration of a sort of dirty rain sweeping across your mask as the sediment is swept along by the tide. But this wasn't as bad as that.

The tide on the wreck, until we learnt how to manage it, was more annoying than the visibility. Safety lines had been trailed from the diving boat above, for if you lost your grip on the wreckage you would surface some distance from the boat and clutching the floating lines saved a long and arduous swim.

Finally I got into the technique of coping with the tide by watching Mike Todd at work. Some of the *Preussen*'s huge ribs still had great strength in them and steel plates still littered the bottom round about. All were covered with mussels and heavily encrusted with other growths.

But they were all strong enough to give a good grip to a gloved hand. So by pulling yourself forward from plate to plate, rib to rib, you could cover the length of the wreck.

There was, of course, nothing of value left – apart from an old gaslight fitting that one diver collected as a souvenir – but it was still interesting to see a wreck for the first time even if she was only in 25 feet of water.

The story of the *Preussen*'s end came from consulting newspaper files and old records at the National Maritime Museum. And it was from that treasure house of records about the sea that the answer came to one thing that had bothered Mike Todd and I about the wreckage.

Every few feet along the greater part of her length were what, at first sight, appeared to be barrels. But the 'barrels' were only barrel-shaped. They were made of solid cement. The answer came from the Museum. Listed in the general cargo of the ship were barrels of cement. The sea had turned them solid.

That was my first wreck. Wrecks it seems were not all that available to me. It was two years before I was to see another in British waters. But that doesn't mean that my diving came to a full stop. Far from it. Bromley Branch was very active and we were always willing to dive.

Not all dives of course were happy affairs with a sense of achievement at the end of them. Our willingness to dive led us into strange and not always happy waters. For example, we cleared wood out of Brooklands Lake for the water bailiff in an attempt to improve the water for the local anglers who were complaining about their lines being snagged on underwater obstructions. We found we were engaged in a major operation far beyond our means. The whole bottom of the lake appeared to be carpeted with timber – and not little pieces at that. Those 45 minutes spent underwater during that dive in nil visibility and maximum depths of 25 feet were really hard work – and then we only cleared a part of the debris nearest to the anglers' favourite fishing spots.

The reason for the amount of timber in the lake was, so we were told, a direct result of wartime camouflage. As it was feared that Brooklands Lake would act as a superb aiming point for German bombers after nearby factories, the surface of the lake was broken up by the means of giant rafts which covered large areas of the water. By this means it was hoped that no moonlight would reflect the shape of the lake to the German bomb-aimers. At the end of the war, the rafts, which were supported by hundreds of oil drums were got rid of in the simplest way.

The drums were holed and the rafts sunk. Now whether this is true or not, someone certainly had dumped vast quantities of wood into the lake. We did our best and a heap of wood on the bank testified to our efforts. So did our aching backs – for the hardest part was hauling the wood ashore once we had pulled one end to the surface.

That dive could hardly be called pleasant, but a really unhappy dive was to follow.

Towards the end of November, 1960, the police appealed to London divers to help them in their search for a fair-haired 12-year-old Girl Guide who was missing from her home in Heston, Middlesex. As secretary of Bromley Branch of the British Sub-Aqua Club I passed on that request to the members of my branch. Other branch secretaries all over London did the same.

The girl's name was Brenda Nash, but at that time the name meant nothing to London divers. Someone wanted their help and they gave it.

At the briefing at Norwood Green police station on Sunday morning November 27, 1960, I got the distinct impression that the police were amazed at the number of divers who responded to their appeal. Over 100 divers stood there in the cold waiting to be told what to do.

Norwood Green police station was no place to brief over 100 of us, so Detective-Superintendent Frederick Hixon, who was in charge of the search for Brenda Nash, called representatives of each group – in most cases it was the branch's diving officer – into the station and told them: 'You will find lots of odd things in the gravel pits we want searched. Concentrate on looking for clothing.'

Branches from all over the area had divers there – Chelsea, Ilford, Hounslow, Uxbridge, Croydon, Bromley had all sent strong groups and there were other branches represented too.

Inspector Robert Epps, himself a keen diver, was seconded from duty in the West End to organise the search and he led the convoy of cars and equipment from Norwood Green to the pits to be searched. Epps was later to head the Metropolitan Police's own special diving team, but at that time this was the biggest mass underwater search ever organised in Britain.

For six hours, 107 divers – three of them were girls – dived in the murk, slime and debris of the gravel pits on either side of Moor-lane, Staines and behind the old Heston Airport.

And it was cold. It was cold changing in the open with only the shelter of a car door to shield you from the wind and it was even colder in the water. Here our wet suits, of course, were invaluable, but so was the training that enabled divers to accept easily the discipline that such a search involved.

At one time the whole of the Bromley Branch contingent were strung out along a line which stretched from bank to bank of one particular pit. The bottom was only 12 feet down, but what a bottom it was. We tried torches, but you could only see them when you put the beam right up to your face. The only way you could see your own fingers was when five blobs appeared pressed against the glass of your mask. And we felt our way along the bottom, which was littered with the debris of everything that anyone had wanted to get rid of at any time in the years since the pits were flooded.

I know at one stage that I found I could go no further forward and finally found that I had my head between the uprights of the head of an old iron bedstead. But we knew when we had finished with that particular pit and some of its unmentionable underwater hazards that the little girl was not there.

I know too that every diver hoped that he (or she) would not find the object of the search and that the little girl would turn up somewhere safe and sound.

The search made front page pictures in all the morning papers the next day, but there was no sign of Brenda Nash. Even then we did not know that this was to turn into one of the classic murder cases of modern times.

The divers had done their best – and the police and hundreds of other land searchers did theirs, but it wasn't until six weeks later that Brenda Nash, still in her Girl Guides uniform, was found murdered under a mound of bracken at Yateley, 25 miles from her home.

The painstaking police work that followed will take its place in the records of detection history. And on June 19th, 1961, Arthur Albert Jones, a 44-year-old fitter-welder, was sentenced at the Old Bailey to life imprisonment for murdering her. All his appeals against the sentence failed.

I don't know what the police records will show to history, but I have the distinct impression that the decision of Scotland Yard to form its own underwater squad was, if not the result of that underwater search, certainly given great impetus by the work of London's amateur divers on that gloomy November day.*

Penny had started taking her diving seriously the previous summer – in fact her log-book started off almost at once recording depths of 65, 65, and 90 feet.

In fact I found that I now had the perfect diving 'buddy'. To be truthful she was very good indeed, passed her tests in rollicking style and in addition to using less air than I did on any one dive – I still reassure myself by saying that women's smaller lungs use less air anyway – seemed much more confident than I had been in the early stages. But then perhaps I was still thinking of the fear that still came upon me at odd times underwater.

When fear hit me – and it seemed to do so with less and less force – any observer could have told you the precise moment of

* The first Metropolitan Police Underwater Search Unit was formed in August 1962 under Inspector Robert Epps of 'C' Division. Epps was a member of the British Sub-Aqua Club long before the formation of the police unit.

the strike. At the moment of the onset of fear I rose about ten feet in the water as though heading for the surface and then I would get the thing under control again and dip down to my original course line.

It is not something of which anyone could be proud, but I am much comforted even now to know that I am not alone in this. Even when watching underwater films of diving experts at work you can sometimes see this reaction – and I know at that moment what made them do it!

Not everyone is fortunate enough to have a diving wife. Off hand I can think of only a few. That expert underwater photographer Geoff Harwood is, for example, blessed with his Jill and there are others. The diver who does not possess such a creature doesn't know what he is missing.

The diving wife doesn't expect you back from a boat trip before you have even thought about your return. She is either out there with you – or knows just how long it takes to get equipment and dive organised and completed. But the real blessing is that she knows what you are talking about and does not need to ask questions all the time to try and establish some sort of idea of the world beneath the surface. She knows, you know.

We began to spend more and more time at Bognor. Not because the town held any particular attraction to us, but because the splendid little yacht club there did. John Messent had joined and bought a boat, not for sailing but for fishing and the enlightened committee of the club didn't frown on this. They felt, and their forward-looking policy has been continued to this day, that anyone who wanted to enjoy the pleasures of the sea was welcome in their club.

So we began to dive regularly at Bognor and I began to think about buying my own boat. Until that happy day John took us out in his.

Penny was now using two little (25 cubic foot) bottles with a Siebe Gorman demand valve centrally mounted on a manifold linking the two. Among divers her bottles were known as 'twin tads' – short for tadpoles – but you'll see very few of them now. The earliest used were war-surplus aircraft cylinders and most of them have now been condemned on safety grounds.

I was using one single (50 cubic foot) cylinder with the

same type of early Siebe demand valve on it. I had bought a twin set of these bottles, but found it so heavy out of the water that I broke it down into two singles. In those days if you had any problems with your demand valve you drove out to the Siebe Gorman works at Chessington and they overhauled it while you watched, but as the number of divers increased Siebe could not continue this sort of all-pals-together service and appointed agents to cope with their servicing.

Our Bognor diving could hardly be called exciting in terms of our diving today, but we thought it was marvellous. We saw pollack and wrasse, oyster shells, the remains of oyster beds, which flourished in ancient times in many places off the coast, bass and cuttlefish and pouting and we thought it wonderful.

The main site for our dives was the Bognor Reef. Really it is more of a place for the spearfisherman for it was rarely over 25 feet deep at the shore end. On low spring tides you can grasp the full extent of the reef by just standing on the shore and looking out to sea. Then a great black carpet of rocks – well, tufts in a carpet really – sweeps away from the shore, out past the pier and on towards the east. At low tide to swim there is like being in an aquarium and not a deep one at that.

Patches of sand and gravel lie between the rock columns and though the brown fronds of laminaria stretch out from the sides and tops of the rocks they often fail to reach to the next rock in the chain. Then a glade opens up – or sometimes a winding channel through the Reef out to the open sea.

It was in one of these glades that Mike Todd, Penny and I saw our first big fish. At first it looked like a piece of corrugated iron on the bottom. I was not surprised to see such a thing, because we were not too far from the shore for man made debris to be a strange sight on the seabed. But when we got closer the piece of 'tin roof' had two big eyes and a long whip-like tail curling away over the sand behind it.

As we got even closer the fish decided it had had enough and it 'took off' from the sand with a great beating of wings. When the turmoil was left behind a great black sting-ray sailed out into clear water. On the sand he had looked four feet across and in action he looked like an aeroplane disappearing into high cloud, which was the limit of our visibility.

Fishermen locally had complained only days before that something had been breaking up their nets and I'm sure that our stingray was the culprit. Apart from the sheer excitement of the sight of him, it provided us with a lot of amusement as we told the story to the Bognor Yacht Club members, exaggerating the size of the fish until one of them said that he was going to keep his feet well out of the water if there was that sort of monster around.

That summer we went to Spain again. This time with Robin and Pauline Messent. Robin took his small Avon inflatable with him. This together with a 3 h.p. Johnson outboard made sure that we were afloat during the week, though we still went out with Francisco and his friends at the week-end.

The inflatable was a howling success and Kevin and Joanna often came along for the ride. We did a lot of diving from the boat. Pauline would look after the children on some secluded beach and Robin, Penny and I would take the boat out on an offshore dive.

But we still didn't understand the Mediterranean. One day trip started off perfectly. We slid over the water until we reached a little cove near Point Bosch down the coast towards Tossa.

Penny, Robin and I went off for a dive. I remember that dive rather well. Though I didn't know it at the time my depth gauge stuck at 30 feet.

The water was gin clear with visibility of over 70 feet. I remember looking up at the surface and thinking how far away it looked for only 30 feet. It wasn't until we got back to the boat that in conversation I found that both Penny and Robin had registered over 60 feet on their depth gauges. And it wasn't until we started heading in for shore that we realised the weather had changed somewhat. It was still baking hot, but there were waves on the beach instead of the glassy calm in which we had set out. I realise now that a tramontana, the unpleasant wind from the north, was obviously just starting up and we hardly noticed it as we were travellling with it as we headed into the beach.

It sounds ridiculous to say now that we had no idea that the boat would be in trouble when we came into land. We jumped out up to our waists and held the boat, which was

Pat Harrison reaches out to give
me a hand through the surf on
our return from my first dive to
over 100 feet. The scene is
Port Salvi Cove, near San Feliu
de Guixols on the Costa Brava.
(*See* Chapter Four)

Volunteers from Bromley Branch take part in the police search for the
body of Brenda Nash at Heston. On the right of the rope is the Branch
diving officer, Bob Murphy; on the extreme left Malcolm Todd, next to
him is the author. *Daily Mail* photograph. (*See* Chapter Seven)

Diver in England: Bernard Rogers after a dive on the Manacles, Cornwall. (*See* Chapter Eleven)

Diver in Spain: The author after a coral dive on th Formigas Islands off the Costa Brava. (*See* Chapte Six)

Penelope in Aiguablava Bay. The house with the slipway running down to the water is that of Senor Martin, guardian of the boats anchored off the hotel. Behind his house is part of the Aigua Blava Hotel itself. (*See* Chapter Ten)

full of equipment, three aqualungs, masks, fins, depth gauges, knives (in sheaths) and my prodder. It was the prodder which was to do the damage. We stood there in the waves for a moment holding the boat and hesitating about dragging it ashore. And at that moment the big wave struck. Or rather it got under the prow of the inflatable and turned it completely upside-down. It was so unexpected that though knocked off our feet by the impact we rather tended to gape at the equipment sloshing about in the waves.

It was a full second or two before I realised that Penny was nowhere to be seen. I scrabbled frantically in the surf at the boat fearing that the aqualung bottles as they were flung over had struck her and knocked her senseless. Heaving the boat upright revealed Penny sitting stunned amid the froth. She had been under the boat, but had somehow escaped being hit by the equipment.

Then we started grabbing equipment and flinging it on to the beach. The only other occupants of that little cove – a Spanish family – joined in the hunt for the equipment. Finally we had it all – except for Robin's sunglasses and we never found those. We were fortunate really, but were now faced with another problem. There would be no return to San Feliu by sea. The inflatable lay limp on the sand. One chamber at least had been pierced by my prodder and there was no repair kit that would cope with a slit like that to be had on a sun-baked Spanish beach. Looking out to sea I was amazed to see white-horses everywhere.

Our problem was, of course, how to get ourselves and all the equipment back to San Feliu. A cliff path fortunately led up to the winding road to Tossa and we managed to hitch lifts back to San Feliu. All of us that is except Robin who stayed with the aqualungs and deflated boat until Francisco came in his boat and picked it all up.

It was a very minor disaster, but it was the first of the lessons we were to receive in the ways of the Mediterranean. The time in which a calm postcard sea can turn into a Hollywood storm epic can be as little as 15 minutes. And the dangers of the Mediterranean are not confined to the weather.

Robin and Pauline had to get back to England, but Penny and I and the children stayed on a little longer. We had several dives and found one or two pieces of old amphora close into the cliffs, but my ambition to find a whole one of these ancient wine jars was still unfulfilled.

The dream of finding an ancient shipwreck and its cargo of amphorae is not confined just to tourist divers. Almost every diver I met on the Costa Brava – and you meet a lot of them when having your bottles refilled at the fine compressor at Paco Carre's boatyard in San Feliu – had the same idea.

The thrill of seeing those ancient jars spilled out over the bottom of the sea is difficult to put into words. Firstly I suppose the actual jar is a mute reminder of people of long ago. It is not some shapeless piece of twisted wreckage that is so often all that remains of a ship. You know what it is, what it was used for (if not wine, perhaps olive oil, or even some spicy mash of fish paste) and that yours is the first hand to touch it since that of some slave or sailor of ancient times.

These graceful pottery jars resist long immersion in the sea and though they are often glibly called the jerricans of the ancient world the description does not really fit. They were used for the same sort of thing – the transport of liquids or near liquids – but they have a line and style that is all their own. Add to that the fact that they can be dated and can often be placed in their exact geographical context and part of the fascination of these jars can be explained.

Divers have always rated these very highly as souvenirs and many a diver's house has a lovingly cared for amphora on a specially-made stand. I can't imagine somehow the same thing being done to a war-surplus jerrican in the years to come – but then you never know!

I know that the archaeologists say that this sort of souvenir hunting may mean the destruction of a site of vast importance to our knowledge of history. I am sure that they are right.

They say, for example, that removing something from a closed time capsule, which is what a wreck really is – you can say with some certainty that everything found in one particular wreck was in use on the day that it sank – may ruin the whole thing.

But this will not stop a diver from taking this sort of souvenir. Nor will weak laws about salvage. Nor will asinine remarks that are attributed to some archaeologists about divers and wrecks. One is said to have remarked: 'We'd rather you didn't find the wrecks at all really, then they'd be there when we can finally get around to dealing with them properly!'

A much more sensible approach that will bring results is that adopted by Joan Du Plat Taylor of Britain's Committee for Nautical Archaeology who believes that divers should be allowed to keep items they find provided they declare them to the archaeologists for examination. If some item is so important that museums must have it then she believes the diver should be paid the proper value of his find.

This sort of deal would do much to stop the black market in antiquities from the sea which certainly exists. It would also do much to stop the similar trade in antiquities that are found on land. It was tried with great success in Cyprus some years ago and the amount of antiquities handed in surpassed the land archaeologists wildest dreams.

But, as I say, all divers dream of finding an amphora. Even my Spanish diving friends. And that dream of old pottery was to lead me within the next few days into a real diving disaster.

Chapter
Eight

Francisco's spearfishing trips had now turned into diving trips and everyone seemed just as keen on looking at fish and the creatures of the sea as they had once been keen on spearing them.

Sometimes I took a heavy metal camera housing with me. This was the prototype of Roy Midwinter's famous Aquasnap perspex case for the Box Brownie. It was ideal for taking pictures in shallow water (pictures good enough for Kodak to put on a window display of some of them), but though it had a flash gun which worked well, the lens of the Box Brownie was not really capable of coping with the difficult lighting at depth. It was also **very** heavy and created weight problems so that you were likely to find your descent speed increasing rapidly the deeper you got.

So most of the time on these dives with Francisco I was content to look rather than record. He had bought an aquaplane and this provided some of the best diving of all. The aquaplane was basically a board with a handle at each end. You gripped these handles and waited while the boat moved off and the rope from the stern to the board straightened out.

Then, as soon as you started to move through the water after the boat, you tilted the board downward – it was shaped rather like an aircraft wing, thicker at the front than the rear – and down you zoomed. Control underwater was simple. Tilt the handles towards you so the board tilted up and up you went. It was a strain on your wrists and arms, and there was quite a danger, if the boat went too fast, of the rush of water ripping your mask off, but, in water of that clarity, it was a thrilling way to search the seabed.

The length of rope decided your ultimate depth of course, but provided you were within that limit, you could swish over rocks, do powered climbs over tall outcrops and then whip down to the seabed again. The number of fish I saw this way was quite extraordinary. The boat would pass overhead and they might take shelter. Once it had passed, out they would come again, only to be 'shot-up' by a board slicing through the water with a diver fluttering at arms' length behind it.

The real problem with using the board was that if you did a steep dive you dare not let go with one hand to squeeze your nose and clear your ears. In this situation you had to pull out of the dive and indulge in some complicated water-batics to get your hand to your mask.

This is, in fact, the trouble with all these aquaplanes. It is all very well zooming through the blue, but unless you can clear your ears by just swallowing – some people can – you have to limit your ups and downs to the amount your ears will take.

If anyone wants to make their own board I can save them a great deal of wasted time. The solution to the ear problem is absurdly simple when you finally think of it. I made my board out of an old occasional table top, fixed two spade handles (quite cheap from a garden supplies shop) at each side, planed down the back end to give it a wing shape, drilled two holes in the leading edge at each side for the rope yoke to go through and then worried about the way to hold the board steady with one hand for about two months.

It was someone who knows nothing about underwater swimming who gave me the idea. 'Couldn't you hook yourself to the board?' he asked. I dismissed the idea at once. The idea of being attached to the board struck me at once as being dangerous. But the word 'hook' stuck in my mind. And then it was easy. Further back from the right handle, but on the same side, I fixed a huge stainless-steel hook to the top surface of my aquaplane.

And that did it. All you have to do when you feel the need to equalise the pressure on your ears is to slip your elbow or forearm under the hook, bring your hand up to your mask, squeeze and then replace your grip on the handle. Instead of the board jerking away as soon as you release one handle, when you have your arm round the hook it stays under control and you can return to full 'flying order' with both hands on the handles at a second's notice.

That aquaplane worked on its first test flight. We were not

so lucky with one that Robin Messent, who had now returned to Spain for diving holidays and I designed on a rather grander scale. This one was intended to take all the strain away from the diver's arms and even had a motor-cycle racing windscreen behind which he could shelter. The idea was that he could lie prone on the machine and by means of an ingenious pair of movable 'wings' – one on each side of the pilot – bank, zoom, and do everything but loop-the-loop. Unfortunately we had not taken into account the fact that such a machine might have a tendency to roll. It did. And it also had a nasty trick of undoing your weight-belt in the middle of its own special tight corkscrew roll!

Several weightbelts later we abandoned the idea for lack of enthusiasm – and lead – and returned to the more primitive model.

But that is not to say that all our ideas didn't work. We decided to make an underwater film – and make it we did. Or rather Robin did. He built the most beautiful solid brass case you have ever seen for a large old-fashioned 16 m.m. cine-camera. It had everything – even a light you could switch on inside to see that all was well and how much film you had left. This worked by a combination of dentists' mirrors and had hours of work put in on that facet alone.

It was very heavy and had to have a large slab of cork floating above it to prevent underwater cameraman and camera plunging headlong into the seabed, but the film was good. Francisco, Juan and Bartolomew acted as diving extras and we photographed dramatic incidents like the struggle to free a giant pinna shell from the seabed.

Seriously, that particular shell – it is like a giant brown mussel and the point is fixed firmly into the seabed – was a struggle. The top end opens when the mussel filters the water through to extract its food, and they normally grow to about a foot long in diveable water, but this one was 26 inches tall.

The reason that divers collect these big mussels is that they are a beautiful mother-of-pearl inside and can be fashioned into highly-decorative lampshades or look beautiful when fixed artistically against a plain white wall.

It is a shame really that they became highly-prized trophies because now you will not find many in shallow water near popular diving areas. The only ones that the divers are likely to have missed are the really well-concealed specimens. Not that they are all that easy to spot at the best of times. They like to anchor themselves deep in the seabed among eel-grass or posidonia weed prairies and often cannot be seen at all from the side because of the surrounding blades of weed. From above they are difficult to spot too. After a time, however, your eye gets accustomed to noticing the dark slit of the open shell when viewed from directly above.

There is a story – well perhaps it is true – that every tenth shell or so contains a natural pearl. To find the pearl you have to sort right through the inside squishy guts of the mussel.

I have never found one, but have seen a shell on the inside of which a piece of grit was being coated with mother-of-pearl. This, of course, is similar to the process by which the oyster forms its pearls, but whether this one would have developed into a pearl it is hard to say. It might well have ended up as just a blister or bump on the pearly inside of the shell. Another thing that you will often find in these big shells is a soft one-clawed crab that makes his home there.

The pinna shell is really the pen shell or fan mussel (pinna aquamosa) and some reference books have it marked down as edible. I have no doubt that it is, but Josef Murla tried one big one that we brought back to the Murla – he is always ready for any gastronomic experience – but pronounced it 'ghastly'.

The pinna shell 'struggle' was only one incident in our filming, of course. But as all photographers will know the really beautiful sights always occurred when we had either left the camera behind or had run out of film the moment before.

So we never captured on film one of the most beautiful sights that I had ever seen underwater up to that time – the slow-motion waltz of three sting-rays.

On this dive we had entered a ravine in the seabed. Near the surface the sides glinted silver-white as the sunlight washed across them in time with the ripples on the surface. Looking through the ravine deeper down the water was an intense, glowing blue – the sort of blue that comes in dreams, but rarely appears on an artist's canvas or the emulsion of a colour film.

The whole effect was one of great beauty, but no action.

The sars that normally add movement to such a scene with their silver sides and black-banded head and tails were missing. So were the saupe, or rather sea bream to give them their proper name.

All was still. But suddenly from one side of the ravine came a stately procession. I don't know if our bubbles or the suck-hiss of our breathing from the demand valves which seemed magnified by the walls about us, had frightened them – or if they were using the ravine as we would a pass through the hills, but, almost in slow motion, along came three sting-rays.

The black bodies were outlined, almost cut-out, against the blue. The two leaders were big, three to four feet across and one was just a nose ahead and below the other. Their 'wings' curled up and down in silent flapping flight.

They were unhurried and after each downward flap the 'wings' curled up and over the body so that the tips almost touched. The long tails, bearing, close to the body, that nasty poisonous barb from which they draw their name, hung down and out behind.

It was slow-motion and beautiful and like a scene from the beginning of the world. They passed some feet away still following one side of the ravine and if they saw us they took no notice. The third member of the group was moving no faster through the water but he had all the appearance of trying desperately to keep up. He was tiny. A miniature of the two that had gone before. It was like a family outing. First went Mummy and Daddy and they along came Junior, scared stiff of being left behind. If sting-rays could talk, this one would have been squeaking desperately – 'Hey, wait for me!'

His frantic haste broke the spell. It was still a wonderful sight, but now it had turned into comedy. We swung round and finned after them. But soon had to turn back as their route led in a long sloping line out of the ravine and down into the deep blue-black ink of the depths.

I never managed either to film Pat Harrison's favourite grouper. This big chap lived in a hole at the foot of the steep slope on one side of Port Salvi cove.

Pat would take parties of his trainees to see the big fish when he felt he could trust them not to disturb it. The fish was brown with yellow markings and could be approached within a few feet if care was taken to avoid kicking up too much fuss on the run-in to his cave.

That grouper was no fool. Each time I tried to get within camera range the fish would be nowhere to be seen. He would obviously have been just as scared of a gun – though the thought of anyone taking a gun to that grouper would have driven Pat Harrison (or Joan for that matter) to apoplexy and without doubt physical violence.

The fish would tolerate a certain amount of watching, but he also had his escape route marked out if the watchers became too pressing. I was a little above and behind the others on one visit to the grouper's castle. From this vantage point I was able to see the emergency exit put into action. While Pat and the other divers peered forward into the gloom, that clever fish was already out of the back door and using a spine of rock as cover slid quietly away behind it.

It was obvious that this particular grouper liked his home very much. About this time work had started on the flats and entertainment complex of swimming pool and night club that is there at San Elmo today.

Pat told me later that the grouper stuck it out to the bitter end. The construction workers disposed of loose rubble into the sea. Gradually this debris tumbled further and further down the underwater slope until it reached the grouper's front door. Still he did not abandon his hole. But finally when the front door was almost completely blocked, he left. One hopes he found a home away from such modern underwater hazards as rubbish dumps.

The modern side of underwater swimming interested me too, of course. Equipment was becoming more and more easily available and reliable. And oddly, enough – or perhaps not when you think about it – as our equipment became more modern I was becoming more and more interested in the past. The past that is that had left its markers on the seabed.

I would not go so far as to say that I was filled with any ambition to become an underwater archaeologist – most archaeologists at that time struck me as being distinctly short-sighted and stuffy about the possibilities under water – but I looked more and more closely at the seabed.

Anything that was even vaguely shaped like pottery received

my full attention. Every underwater magazine I looked at seemed full of ancient objects recovered by divers – the ancient amphorae were everywhere judging by those pictures.

For a long time I never found a whole one. Francisco told me that divers had found a lot near Tossa and that there were vague reports of some near where we dived each week-end with his friends.

I kept thinking I saw them. But each time I dived down to look at my find it turned out to be an oddly-shaped rock or twisted stone. From above the seabed is full of such deceits. The real test is, of course, a close approach, but after a while your eyes learn to discard most rocks at once. Things that are man-made have angles and curves that nature rarely copies though of course there are exceptions to that simple rule.

It is strange now to think that all the time we were going off on these diving trips we were passing over one deposit of pottery within moments after starting out.

I am not referring to the rocks within feet of the shore on the right-hand side inside San Feliu harbour – though there within inches of the feet of surface swimmers from the crowded beach there are many pieces of ancient pottery, but rather to the little passage between the Island of Freu and the headland of St Elmo that we ran the boat through on our way down the coast towards Tossa.

Just there, under a modern concrete gun emplacement built for a reason I am never quite sure about (did Spain think she would have to defend the ports of the Costa Brava against Germany? Or France? In World War Two?) on a steep slope of fallen boulders you can find the handles of Phoenician amphoras in water some 70 feet deep. But I cannot tell if these are the traces of a shipwreck of ancient times.

It could be that they were thrown over the cliff long ago. It could also be that a Phoenician trader anchored there out of the wind and decided to clean ship and dump the broken wine jars over the side. This last was apparently a common practice in days long ago, for the ships then could do little against a head-on wind and would anchor in some sheltered spot and do a bit of tidying up. The headlands of many Mediterranean coasts bear witness to this because abandoned anchors are found in great quantities on the seabed below the cliffs.

This interest in amphorae was an addition to the thrill of normal diving. But it was also to bring us close to tragedy...

The day started so well. An early start. A calm sea and sun. And a morning of diving in front of us. We joked together as we went along the coast towards Point Bosch and Canyet. Francisco had heard of a possible site of an ancient shipwreck. Someone had seen what they thought were amphorae on the seabed, but had been unable to reach them because they were short of air.

Excited though I was at the possibility of finding a complete amphora at last, there was a suggestion of depth about this statement that I didn't really like. I made a private resolve that, amphora or no amphora, I would call off the dive if it got too deep.

Soon we were over the spot. This time, instead of the usual practice of Julian keeping the boat near the divers, we anchored. I knew from the amount of anchor rope that went out that this was a deep one. Francisco and Paco Carre, who runs the boatyard and compressor at the back of San Feliu harbour, were first into the water. I set my watch and followed them. The anchor rope went straight down – a shining bar of golden-brown near the surface with air bubbles still clinging to the rough weave, shading to bubbleless brown and darker brown further down.

I went down it hand over hand, stopping every now and then to clear my ears. The visibility didn't seem all that good for at 80 feet I could still not see the bottom, just the rope stretching on down. Francisco and Paco must, I thought, be much, much deeper, judging from the chandelier of white fizz from their expired air that streamed past me a few feet away from the rope. I went down another few feet. Still no sign of the bottom. This was not going to be much of a dive for me. At the rate I was using air I would just about have time to reach the bottom and then come straight up again.

I decided to call it off and save some of my air for a dive in shallower water. I rose slowly up towards the glow of the sunlight and then angled in towards the shore in search of a more reasonable depth. I swanned around for a bit and then returned to the boat. In doing so I used up almost all my air.

Bartolomew had gone directly to shallower water and was still under.

When Francisco came to the surface, I glanced at my watch. 32 minutes. I was worried about the time he had spent at a depth that must be over 120 feet. He didn't appear to have decompressed on the way up – and I felt sure that he should have done even though I hadn't got my decompression tables with me.

To my horror instead of climbing out of the water he reached into the boat, took a diving torch and disappeared under the water again. At that moment I realised that he was going back down again.

I reset my watch and cursed the stupidity that had made me leave the diving tables behind. Now it was certain that unless Francisco and Paco decompressed they must be running a great risk of the diver's disease, the bends.

The bends are named after the twisting of limbs that can take place as a direct result of inadequate decompression. Basically what happens is that while the diver is underwater the air he breathes is under great pressure too. Both life-giving oxygen and neutral nitrogen in that air are absorbed into the bloodstream. The nitrogen must be given time to come out of solution slowly. This is done by means of a slow ascent and then the nitrogen comes out of solution and is breathed away from the tissues of the lungs. Come up too quickly after a long period of nitrogen absorption at depth and the nitrogen emerges, not as tiny bubbles that the tissues can cope with, but in bubbles big enough to collect at the joints and cause crippling pain.

The effect of a rapid ascent is often compared, in its effect in the bloodstream, with taking the top off a bottle of lemonade. The bubbles that then appear are the direct result of the removal of the cap and the release of pressure.

Both Francisco and Paco appeared after another 15 minutes. But both seemed quite unconcerned with my pleas for them to decompress. They gave the impression that they thought I was making a fuss about nothing.

Within a short while even before we had really started on the way back to San Feliu, Francisco started rubbing his knees and complaining of an 'aching'. Paco reported no such symptoms.

Reluctantly Francisco was persuaded to put on my aqualung and to decompress for as long as the air lasted. To do this we headed the boat into shallow water and sent him down to the bottom at what appeared on the depth gauge to be exactly 20 feet. When he had used up my air, we swapped him on to what was left of Bartolomew's bottle but it was hardly more than enough for a few drags. Once again I cursed the lack of diving tables, but now their presence would not have helped. There was no more air left in the boat.

For a while Francisco felt better. The pain in his knee had disappeared and he was inclined to scoff at my unhappiness about the whole affair. He said that they had been between 37 and 40 metres for the whole dive. They had not seen the amphorae, but there was a big cave down there. Which was why he had come up for the torch.

Though Francisco felt better, I kept urging that when we got back to harbour we should get some more bottles and he should undergo more decompression, but it was clear that both he and Paco thought this completely unnecessary.

All went well until we were actually crossing the harbour and heading for Paco's boatyard. Then I noticed that Francisco was rubbing his elbow in a rather puzzled way.

As we came alongside the quay, I again suggested further decompression, but I was now beginning to feel like the spectre at the feast and accepted without protest their refusal. 'It's nothing,' said Francisco, 'nothing that an aspirin and a hot bath won't cure . . .'

We parted at the gateway to the boatyard and Francisco walked off back to his house apparently quite all right. I went back to the Hotel Murla and joined Penny for pre-lunch drinks. I told her what had happened and got out the diving tables to find out just how much decompression they should have done.

Francisco's dive even though it was interrupted by his ascent for the torch must certainly be counted for the complete time of the two descents together. I was dismayed to find that at the very least he should have stopped at 30 feet for five minutes, another five minutes at 20 feet and a full 25 minutes at 10 feet.

In fact all he had was a measly 12 minutes at 20 feet. Though it was probably better than nothing it seemed very little.

Yet, I told myself, he had seemed all right when we parted. And Paco Carre had no trouble at all. Perhaps I was making a bit of a fuss over nothing. At the same time I resolved that I would never go out again without the diving tables safely in my diving bag. And I would take great care when diving deep. The Mediterranean makes it very easy for a diver to revel in its clear waters and forget all about the depth he is at and the time he is there.

So I almost forgot about it over lunch and the wine and the food soon sent me to my bed for a siesta.

I was woken by a knocking on our door. Grabbing some swimming trunks for the sake of decency I opened it to find Josef Murla standing there. 'Francisco is not well,' he said. 'It is something to do with the diving. They want to see you.'

There was no more to the message than that. The very shortage of information I found ominous. I dressed and hurried out into the hot stale air of the Calle Mayor. By the time I reached Francisco's house I was sweating heavily, but the sight I found as I pushed through the open door at the top of the stairs chilled me.

Francisco was lying on the floor. His knees appeared to be drawn up towards his chin and though he greeted me from this strange position cheerfully enough there was not the slightest doubt that he was in pain.

Paco Carre was there. So, I was glad to see, was Pat Harrison. The other man present was obviously the doctor. He was obviously worried and I felt for him because this was probably the first case of bends he had ever seen in his life. Yet he was eminently sensible and was listening carefully to a translation of what Pat Harrison was saying. 'He's got to be recompressed,' said Pat and then went on to explain simply what the trouble was.

There was only one problem. Where was the nearest decompression chamber? There was some talk of one higher up the coast towards the French frontier.

This was discarded because nobody really had any firm information about it. Was it open? Where exactly was it? Was a doctor available? No one knew for certain.

I looked at Pat who stood the other side of Francisco's recumbent form. 'It's Barcelona,' said Pat firmly . . . 'The C.R.I.S. Club centre. They're fully equipped. It's the only thing to do.'

He was, of course, right. And from the look of Francisco it had be better be quick. Pat suggested taking his Land-Rover but it was obvious that my Vanguard shooting brake would make better time.

Once that was decided and decisions came fast in this situation, I ran back to the Murla and the car. Only stopping long enough to borrow some petrol money from the bar in the front of the hotel from Ramon and to give him a message for Penny, I roared the car back to Francisco's.

I seemed to be outside the house for only a moment before Francisco was lifted into the back, his wife scrambled in beside him and Paco jumped in beside me. One of the crowd promised to ring the C.R.I.S. headquarters and warn them that we were on the way. And then we were off.

After nearly hitting a stupid woman tourist at the exit to the town as she stepped off the pavement without looking, I tried to calm down and concentrate on getting the maximum speed with the minimum of risk. But I knew that Francisco was in a bad way and I felt that every minute was one too many.

Chapter
Nine

The Vanguard crashed and thudded in and out of potholes until I feared that the whole front suspension would come adrift, but I kept my foot down.

I had been into Barcelona by car only once before and after that trip from San Feliu, there and back, I swore I would never use a car of mine on that road again. Compared with today's modern road, the old route was a cart-track. It was narrow and in many places the edges were worn away around the roots of the big trees that crowded the two-lane traffic towards each other. Cart-track is the right description for carts still used it and their iron-rimmed wheels had cut away the tarmac that the sun had melted into waves and hummocks.

At a sensible speed for those conditions the 67-mile journey took almost four hours and even then your hands were sore at the end from the yammering of the steering wheel. There was plenty of traffic from ancient Spanish lorries laden with farm produce and the more modern French lorry and trailer combinations to cars of all shapes and sizes and right on down to motor-cycles and push bikes. All this traffic from the Spanish border and back to it was funnelled in and out of Barcelona by the one road. And sections of it, through coastal villages, were major hold-ups. At these traffic was one-way and controlled by lights.

This time it was the Vanguard's turn to be tested and, though it was one of the toughest cars I know, I had my doubts when a great hole appeared right in front of the offside wheel and the steering kicked so violently that it almost got away from my sweating hands. The suspension bottomed with a grinding thump and I thought we had lost a wheel, but the car came upright with a convulsive lurch and then the whole thing was repeated with the rear wheel. My whole body tensed as the rear wheel went in and it was almost as though I was physically hurt by the noise. I liked that car.

Paco Carre, who sat beside me, muttered something in French for my benefit about it being a strong car, but I knew we would have to ease down. There was no point in bumping Francisco around like that or in breaking down before we could reach the recompression chamber. The miles into Barcelona stretched endlessly ahead in my mind and I was torn between the need for speed and the need to get there in one piece.

In the back Francisco's wife kept him as comfortable as she could and said something to Paco. But it was Francisco who told me what she said.

'We must stop soon, Kendall,' he said, 'I have to take the medicine in water.'

Though he spoke perfectly rationally and calmly his condition was obviously not good. Every now and then a muttered curse and groan would come from him as the twinges of the bends caught him. I knew enough to know that if he was not recompressed soon the nitrogen bubbles that were being released from his bloodstream and were swelling in his joints causing intense pain, could move to his heart – and kill.

The doctor, though he obviously knew very little about the bends, had realised this and had prescribed drops from a little bottle of digitalis to act as a heart stimulant during the journey.

I pulled off at a crowded roadside restaurant and Francisco's wife went running to get a glass of water. I could see her struggling to get attention from the harassed waiters. I sat and sweated and fumed. The car-park was crowded with Barcelona people returning from Sunday excursions and the traffic was getting heavier and heavier by the minute.

We waited there, a little island of trouble in the middle of happy unconcerned people. Nobody cared. And to be fair they had no way of knowing of our particular problem.

This feeling that nobody cared grew on me once we were back on the road and back to speed. I couldn't see Francisco in my rear-view mirror as he was lying on the seat. But I knew things were not getting any better when he had the nearside rear window opened so that he could stretch his feet out. The bends seemed to relax for a time and then his feet would be back inside and I could imagine him in the knees drawn-up position that I had first seen him in on the floor of his house.

I was getting so desperate now about the amount of traffic that I was running down the outside of the Barcelona-bound stream sounding my horn almost continuously in the hope that people would realise we were in trouble. But nobody cared. One by one they would try to challenge me until oncoming cars would have to hug the trees in desperation to get out of the way of the maniac in the centre of the road with the equally stupid driver on the inside who refused to give way to a lunatic foreigner in a hurry.

More than once I had to brake viciously to avoid a crash. I prayed desperately that we would be stopped by one of the motor-cycle Spanish policemen who seemed to haunt every mile of road on the days you didn't want them.

But there were no policemen on motor-bikes that evening. Paco tried fluttering a white handkerchief out of his window on the offside. He told me to sound my horn in regular short hoots and said that this was the recognised signal for a car in distress on the Continent and in Spain in particular. But it had no effect. Passengers in the car in front would crane round to see what the matter was and then speak to the driver. You could almost see determination not to be passed – as well as two little horns – sprout from the back of the driver's head. And another race for supremacy was on.

In the end I stopped sounding the horn and found I had more chance of passing the middle of road mimser if I sneaked up on him quietly and was past in a rush of air before he had time to wind his car up to contest speed.

Even so the drive into Barcelona seemed endless and another hazard was added. The light began to fail and under the narrow lane of trees it was dark. Lights blazed out and I was fortunate that I had fitted yellow bulbs.

What the reaction to my headlong plunge through the darkness would have been if my lights had been white, I shudder to think. It was bad enough to be flashed at for being too far over on the wrong side while overtaking, but if I had also done it with white headlights every oncoming driver would have given me the benefit of his full beams for sure.

I began to indulge in fantasies in which with one policeman

ahead and one behind – both with howling sirens – the whole road was cleared into Barcelona for me.

But it was not to be. Close shave followed close shave and still the car stood up to the battering. Thinking back on it, it was quite clear that the reason I got past so much traffic was not pure driving skill, but the fact that I was willing to submit the car to the punishment of that terrible surface.

The closer we got to Barcelona the heavier the traffic. Through the seaside resorts on the way – a mass of lights and howling canned music – the traffic slowed to a walking pace. My only chance of making progress was outside the towns and the closer to the city the closer together the resorts became. Only the brakes saved us between Premia de Mar and Masnou.

We had stopped talking long ago and when the brakes locked and we skidded on the slippery melting surface out of the way of the oncoming car I had a brief glimpse in the headlights of Paco's face – eyes screwed up against the headlights and tension there in every shadow of the yellow light.

I wondered how I looked. My arms and back ached. And then I felt ashamed thinking of that sort of tiredness compared with Francisco. God knows what he was going through in the back.

Suddenly from the darkness behind me, he said : 'If it were done it had better be done swiftly – but Kendall don't kill us all on the way!' And he laughed. It was the most comforting sound I had heard in the whole trip. In the bounce-back from the headlights I could see Paco's teeth show white for a moment and I grinned too. He couldn't be that bad, surely, if he could quote Shakespeare at me!

At the next town – I think it was Mongat – we came to an abrupt halt. The traffic through the town was one way and the queue ahead of me trying to get into Barcelona seemed endless. I couldn't even see the traffic light which was holding us up.

We crawled forward an inch at a time. And there, suddenly, was my motor-cycle cop! He sat on his bike almost in the shadows cast by a neon sign watching the traffic crawl past him.

'Paco!' I pointed to the policeman. Paco was out of the car in a flash and running to the policeman. An animated conversation took place between them with much arm-waving and pointing on Paco's part as I slowly crawled with the traffic towards them.

At first the policeman looked disinterested. Then he jerked into life, kicked his engine over and rode off down the outside of the queue. Paco came back and jumped in while we were still moving slowly on.

He said something very fast in Catalan to the darkness at the back of the car. I didn't understand a word. Then he tried me in French, but that didn't make much sense either. We sat looking at one another in the odd blue light from the neon sign and I suddenly felt too tired to even try to understand. Why hadn't the policeman waved us out to follow him? Why after all this time when we finally found someone who could help us didn't he stick with us and clear the way?

I was suddenly conscious of being very very hot. My shirt stuck to me everywhere. I could feel a pool of sweat that seemed only held up by my waistband. I took several deep breaths because I felt just as though the air was not doing me any good. The smell of cooking nearby seemed to add to the heat and I felt a little giddy.

Francisco's wife was saying something in French. It sounded like 'the agent has gone to change the light'. Understanding stirred slowly. I was almost there when Francisco said in English 'The policeman has gone to change the light.'

The traffic light! Of course. The motor-cycle Guardia had gone to change the traffic light in our favour. It was the most sensible and intelligent thing to do. It would be no good leading me into the one-way and meeting a gigantic lorry head on. The sensible thing to do was to stop the oncoming traffic and let us through.

Shortly afterwards we were on the move again. Full marks to the policeman on the N.2. My only disappointment was that he did not drive ahead of us and help us with the rest of the traffic, but you can't have everything.

It didn't seem to take long after that. The traffic was all bowling along at what seemed a ridiculously fast speed on the main approach road to the city.

In the great open squares of Barcelona it was cooler and the relief of having made it added to my loss of tiredness.

Francisco insisted on sitting up despite the pleas of his wife. Now all we had to do was to find the right place.

What we were looking for was the depot of the famous Spanish diving club – the Centro de Recuperacion Investigaciones Submarinas – in the Conde de Asalto, where the recompression chamber was installed.

We stopped and asked various people. All were helpful and finally one pedestrian gave us precise directions. One last near miss – when a car shot across my bonnet in a dark square. And suddenly we were there – only to find it in darkness and all shuttered and barred. Someone had misunderstood the message. Instead of arriving to find everything ready to recompress Francisco right away, there was no one there at all.

The building had a sort of corrugated steel shutter covering the whole front. It is the sort of thing that slides up and down and covers many a shop front at night. I suppose the Depot used to be a shop – on the other hand it may well have been designed that way to facilitate the movement of heavy equipment in and out.

Whatever it was, the place was shut and locked. Thundering on the steel shutters produced a head of a woman out of an upstairs window and a shouted conversation between Paco and the woman soon produced some action.

I must congratulate the C.R.I.S. Club on their efficiency. Within a very short time the shutters were open and Francisco was helped inside.

I revised the opinion I had gained from his brave remarks in the car when I saw him lying on the cushions on the floor as people fussed around the huge bank of cylinders which were to provide the pressure for his decompression.

We had made the run in not much over three hours – a record – but under the harsh neon tubes of the recompression centre there was not the slightest doubt that Francisco was in pain, indeed had been in pain the whole trip. The dark rings around his eyes testified to that.

'Don't look so sad, Kendall,' he said looking up at me from the floor. Sad? I could have cried. What had started out as a happy diving trip had ended like this. Or rather had not yet ended. I tried to smile at him and said something like 'Sad, me? Never!,' but sadness was not the word for the misery I felt.

Any diver who shrugs off the bends as something minor and an exaggerated risk should have been with me then. Any diver who thinks he can pare down the decompression tables to suit his own convenience should have been with me then. The bends – even for an onlooker – are not a subject to treat lightly.

Paco Carre looked just as worried as I did. He had done exactly the same dives as Francisco yet he was not suffering at all. Why should it strike one and not the other?

Paco's frame was fractionally better covered than Francisco's. And all I had read suggested that Paco should have been more likely to have suffered from the bends than Francisco.

Why didn't he? I have discussed this with Royal Navy diving experts like Surgeon Rear-Admiral Stanley Miles, and they all stress that no one can be sure how any one person will react to incorrect diving.

The recompression chamber – a one man affair scarcely bigger than a man's body into which the person to be recompressed is slid on the back – was being made ready.

A little window of super-strong plate glass is set near the head end of the steel tube so that the victim can be observed at all times. The technique employed by the Spanish divers was to instruct the diver being recompressed to give the O.K. sign used underwater – the thumb and forefinger of the right hand are linked to make the signal – all the time while in the chamber. They can then tell immediately if the victim becomes unconscious or if the return to the 'surface' on releasing the pressure in the chamber is causing pain. If it does the pressure inside the chamber is increased and the diver is taken 'down' again and brought 'up' more slowly. In other words the whole idea is to simulate the conditions of the dive with a much slower return to the surface than actually took place.

This slow return to the surface allows the nitrogen to emerge from the bloodstream slowly in the form of tiny bubbles which do no damage to the joints. Francisco's trouble was that the bubbles had become big and were collecting at the joints causing intense pain. By increasing the pressure and taking him 'down again below the depth he had reached on the real dive – the bubbles could be compressed again. Then by a long slow 'ascent' the bubbles would be released in a reduced form and he should have slid out of the chamber completely cured.

There was just one snag. As the C.R.I.S. divers had not been alerted, the diving doctor to supervise the recompression was nowhere to be found! Our troubles were not over.

I was commandeered to drive people all over Barcelona to find the doctor. At fashionable restaurant after fashionable restaurant heads were shaken. He was not there. Finally he was located by someone else and without the slightest hesitation he gave up his dinner and raced to the C.R.I.S. depot. Seconds after we returned from our fruitless search, Francisco was being slid into the chamber to start his long recompression.

There was nothing I could do. Once or twice I looked in through the little glass plate and grinned reassuringly at him – and he grinned back, behind the fixed O.K. sign of his fingers.

Any hope that the decompression schedule would be a short one was gone when, after pumping Francisco down to below his diving depth, they tried to bring him back very slowly to surface pressure. His contorted face showed only too clearly through that little pane of glass that the pain was back. The Spanish diving-doctor immediately ordered a return to depth and, with a sigh that was almost audible the C.R.I.S. club members settled down for a long night.

There was nothing I could do to help. And I felt helpless. Francisco's wife and I conversed in shockingly bad French and went round the corner to a little café to eat. But neither of us felt hungry and were soon back in the neon-tube light and the bare walls of the room that housed the one-man decompression chamber. Outside Barcelona settled down for a hot still night. Inside the room stark white light left few shadows and seemed to focus all attention on the grey steel tube in the centre of the floor.

It seemed so stark that it was difficult to realise that there was a man inside. There was little noise. Every now and then the compressor would start up to supply more air to the storage cylinders.

The Spaniards showed me another side to their characters in those long drawn out hours of stress. No one could describe them as a quiet people. They are given to noise as naturally as their sun is given to heat. But now they went about the job of attending a stricken diver with the sort of coolness and quietness that one does not usually associate with Latins.

No one there at that time could ever accuse the Spanish again of being a *mañana* people. When it mattered they were quiet and efficient. But then perhaps I was watching the true Catalan at work. There are good grounds for saying that the Catalan is not typical of the whole of Spain. Spanish, yes, but not typically Spanish – the sort of Spaniard that the tourist brochures would have you believe does nothing but sleep in the noon-day sun.

Yet the atmosphere of cool calm efficiency was not altogether uplifting. Somehow the tube of the recompression chamber began to take on the aspect of a coffin as it lay there in the centre of the stage. I prayed that it would not be and was shaken out of this sort of thought by the sight of the man leaning over the little glass window, concentrating completely on Francisco lying there underneath him. There was no thought of death in that man's face; quite the contrary, calm reassurance was written clear in his expression.

The dive and the drive were beginning to take their toll of me. I began to ache for sleep. But I had yet one more part to play. Seated on a box to the right of the recompression chamber was a high official of the C.R.I.S. Club. Seated facing him was Paco Carre. An investigation was obviously in progress. Question from the stern face of the investigator. Answer from the worried face of Carre. My Spanish, as I have said before is bad, my Catalan impossible. But there was no doubt at all as to the reason for all the questions. How did this happen? And from the answers one could only hope that some unknown diver would avoid the mistake that had put Francisco in that steel cylinder nearby.

I was jerked into wakefulness by a courteous request to take my place before the investigator. Did I speak Spanish? A little. But it was obviously not enough for the questions that followed. A switch to French. A little better. Now the questions flowed thick and fast. How deep? How long? How much decompression? Why not longer?

And under the heading of 'Declaracion de Señor Don Kendall McDonald' it was all carefully written down.

How long were they under for the second dive? My mind

refused to function. And then I remembered my diving watch. I had set it at the time of the second dive because I was so worried about the length of time they had been under. And there, clear before my eyes was the setting still in place. I showed my watch explaining what had happened. And then it was all over. My statement was on the record. The Spanish written record was an example to anyone involved in a similar incident – except that dive times should all have been written down at the time of the actual dive and then there would have been no need for the recall of tired memories.

Certainly efficiency seems to go hand in hand with the C.R.I.S. Club. Somewhere on their records is the story of that dive. A record that will help to stop it happening again.

I could hardly keep my eyes open any longer. I didn't want to leave Francisco lonely in his pain, but more knowledgeable people than I were now completely in charge. I went out to the car and for a moment the nip in the air compared with the heat of a few hours before revived me. I sat in the car seat and slowly gave way to tiredness.

I dreamed unmentionable things about diving, but awoke to a hand shaking my shoulder. It was Francisco's wife, who must have been awake the whole time.

I sat up. During my sleep I had slipped sideways on to the passenger seat and my whole body ached from the uncomfortable position I had adopted. When sense stirred through my awakening I slid out and shivered in the chill dawn air. It was five a.m. and Francisco appeared at the doorway supported by men on either side. He grinned at me weakly and seemed unsteady on his feet.

An ambulance waited and with Paco Carre we followed to the hospital. Francisco was to be detained for a day to make sure there were no ill effects. One of his ankles was painful but apart from that he seemed in good spirits.

We followed him into the quiet corridors of the hospital. And then he was gone into the care of the doctors and nurses. There was nothing more to do. His wife was staying the night, so Paco and I turned and went out to the car.

The morning light got stronger and stronger as we drove back. We bought and drank a fizzy drink of some kind from a lonely, but open garage, filled up with petrol with the money Ramon Murla had lent me, and then headed back towards San Feliu.

Somewhere on that journey we stopped. The sun was up, but the Mediterranean looked grey and cold. At that moment I hated it, and I felt I would never dive again.

Chapter
Ten

Though Francisco was only detained overnight, he was weakened by his ordeal. The hours of lying in that little metal tube waiting for the pain to return each time they tried to bring him back to atmospheric pressure were, let's face it, enough to weaken even the strongest mind and body.

The decompression routine (five hours and a pressure equivalent of 170 feet) had undoubtedly saved his life, but he was not to escape scot-free. To this day one of his ankles is almost devoid of feeling and for some time he limped as he walked.

Even so he was incredibly cheerful about the whole thing. What astounded me was the fact that though he had been diving for some time he confessed he knew little at that time about the need for decompression by means of a slow ascent and special stops before breaking through the surface.

His accident put an end, of course, to our boat trips, but it put an idea into Francisco's mind that he broached to me on the day before we left San Feliu at the end of our holiday.

'Why,' he said, 'don't you have a boat of your own built here?'

I laughed. 'How often do I have to tell you,' I said, 'that just because we have a car and come on holidays abroad that we are not millionaires.' We had this standing joke about the amount of money tourists earned ever since years ago when we first met Juan Auladell who asked me how much my car cost. When I told him he had converted it into pesetas and then remarked slightly bitterly that the car had cost more than he earned in a whole year even working at two jobs.

'No, I'm serious,' said Francisco – 'I could get you a boat with engine for about 15,000 pesetas.' Now it was my turn to do a quick calculation. It worked out at about £90. I assumed he was talking about a second-hand boat and said so.

'No, no,' said Francisco as though I was daft, 'built for you.

Just like my boat. Twenty-four palms (the Spanish measure boats by the spread hand in somewhat the same way we talk of a horse being so many hands high). The engine would be second-hand of course.'

'Of course,' I said wondering still whether he was having me on.

But he wasn't and I handed over the major part of the money so that the boatbuilder, Señor Jose Camprubi, could buy the wood and start work that winter.

Penny and I wondered on our return to London whether we had done the right thing. It would, of course, be lovely to have a boat of our own in Spain, but at that time it was a large investment and brought our total capital down to nil.

No one could call Francisco the world's greatest letter writer – he always wrote to us in English and it must have been a great effort as he worried a great deal about the correct grammar – but that winter he surpassed himself.

Every now and then a letter would arrive with a picture of the work so far. A page from a calendar would be pinned to the ribs of the boat and so we could see the work progressing as the calendar moved closer and closer to the time to think about another holiday. In the foreground of the picture would be Señor Camprubi and his grin was absolutely full of confidence. As he seemed always to be working with the minimum of tools – an adze and a plane seemed his principal instruments – his progress seemed fantastic.

As the day of our departure for San Feliu drew closer and closer Penny and I would discuss possible names for the boat, but by the time we left though we had one or two fanciful ideas – Rascasse (after the scorpion fish) was high on the list – nothing was settled.

The reality of the boat exceeded our wildest dreams. She was magnificent. From her gleaming white hull to the decorative red line round her bulwarks, she was perfect. The high pointed prow was very Spanish fishing boat – what else would it be! – and I noted that it was painted red. This reminded me of an article I had read only a short time before about the ships of ancient days. It was customary to sacrifice a ram or sheep before setting off on a voyage and daub the blood and mount the head on the ship's prow. It is for this reason that many boats in the Mediterranean today have a splash of red colouration near their bows – a hangover from the ancient past.

But I had little time to think of that. The stern even had varnished wood where you sat to handle the tiller. The petrol tank was mounted inside a wooden casing on the right hand side of the bow and two hatches which interlocked, gave access to the engine.

The engine itself was second-hand, but you wouldn't have been able to tell it. It was a 4 h.p. Solzan and it's workings were a bit of a mystery to me. The solitary plug was mounted on top of an ignition chamber and it seemed clear that the cylinder went across from side to side.

The gearbox behind the engine was empty of gears – they were always going to be fitted but never finally were – so the boat went forward or stopped; there was no reverse or neutral. This made swinging her a bit of an effort until you got the knack of it and in a crowded anchorage it made life a bit hazardous.

But to me she was – and always will be even now she has been sold – a perfect boat to own.

The day we launched her, slings were put underneath her and Paco Carre's latest acquisition – a swivelling crane – lowered her gently into the water. She floated perfectly in trim which when you consider the hand-and-eye building of her was a magnificent achievement.

Francisco took us for a trip round the harbour and then handed her over to me. I was a bit overwhelmed particularly when I couldn't get her to start! The small crowd on the quay nearly died laughing at my efforts. Sweat streamed down me in the heat as I swung and swung that engine.

The engine became less cursed when someone on the quay took pity on me and let me in on the joke. There was a tap near the bow, inside the hatch and just under the petrol tank which turned the petrol on and off. It was off and one swing after turning it on started the engine. I was happy again and master of the ship.

But I was master of a ship without a name. I talked to Francisco about it. He didn't think much of any of the names I suggested. Then someone else told me that the Marine Commandant at that time had been badly shocked by a translation of some of the names of the tourist's boats that were moored in his harbour. The French, in particular, were rather keen, it seemed, on risqué names for their boats – though I must say in retrospect that by the standards of today's permissive society they were all exceptionally tame. Not that the permissive society has even yet reached Spain, nor, in some ways, do I hope that it will.

The Marine Commandant it seemed was rather keen on boats that had the names of Saints on them. I jibbed hard at this. To call a boat by the name of a Saint seemed to me like snivelling before you were hurt. Though I believe in God it did seem like hitting below the belt to ask for Divine Intervention and give a boat a religious name.

I felt too that God is not mocked to judge by the history of wrecks. Take the Spanish Armada as a simple example. Religious names had not saved many of them. In particular I thought of the Santa Maria de la Rosa, which some friends of mine were trying hard to find in the stormy waters of the Blasket Sound in Ireland (Sydney Wignall has at the time of writing located her and is conducting a serious underwater archaeological investigation of her remains).

Then Francisco had his great idea. 'What is your wife's name?' he asked as though he didn't know it.

'Penelope.'

'That's it,' he said, 'Santa Penelope, the Saint of Patience. We shall call her Santa Penelope.'

'We shall do no such thing,' I replied. But on second thoughts it was the perfect name without the Saint part. So *Penelope* she became.

Penelope opened up a new field of diving to us. With your own boat you can explore all sorts of inaccessible spots. And though she would only do five knots flat out we could go anywhere we wanted at any time the sea condition would allow.

But before we had left England to enjoy *Penelope* to the full I was involved in two projects which increased my diving experience. The first like that unhappy dive for Brenda Nash, was a search for a missing child.

This time the youngster was a ten-year-old Wolf Cub called Billy Holloway of Hayes. He had disappeared on the evening of St Valentine's Day, in February 1962. And the police began a massive search ... door to door and in the fields and in derelict buildings around his home. On one day alone some 2,000 men, women and children searched in biting winds and flurries of snow, but found no trace of the missing boy.

Police frogmen searched the River Crane and Detective Chief Supt. Denis Hawkins, one of the Yard's Big Five, and Det. Supt. Roland Brickett of 'X' Division C.I.D., who were in charge of the case, ordered a minute search of flooded gravel pits, streams, rivers and the Grand Union Canal.

This was where Bromley Branch of the British Sub-Aqua Club took part in the search for little Billy. This time there was no concentration of divers in one spot, but little groups of amateurs were allocated to the various gravel pits around the area. On February 25, Bromley Branch were allocated Dawley Gravel Pits and the morning dawned even colder than that of the Brenda Nash search. By the time we got into the water there was powdered snow all over the banks of the pits and the visibility underwater was so appalling that Bob Murphy, our branch diving officer, ordered rope links between each pair of divers.

We found the bottom by pawing at it with frozen, though gloved hands, and by what feeling we had the bottom of our particular pit was of firm mud studded with large stones. We did our best, but as a methodical search it was a failure. We just had not got enough divers to ensure that we had covered the whole bottom. Even so it was fair to say that it was unlikely, though not impossible, that we would have missed a body on the bottom. If that body had been in some way floating in mid-water, however, we would certainly not have found it.

To give you some idea of how cold it was: two demand valves froze up after the divers had surfaced for only a few minutes. The water, of course, as is often the case in extremely low temperatures was warmer than the surrounding air. Changing out of wet-suits with ice on them was in those circumstances sheer misery, but the landlord of a local pub was kind enough to let us use a shed in his yard for the last stage of complete exposure.

A month after he disappeared Billy Holloway was found dead in the muddy waters of the Grand Union Canal at Seven Mile Bridge, Hayes. It was only a mile from his home and only 400 yards from the spot that he was last seen alive. In April, 1962, an open verdict was returned at the Ealing inquest and the West Middlesex Coroner, Mr H. D. Broadbridge said that there was no evidence to show how the lad came to be in the water.

My second new diving experience was a trip to the mouth of the Thames and one of the anti-aircraft defence towers, which were later to become famous as the homes of the 'pop pirates'. As a dive, despite glowing reports of fantastic visibility and a plethora of lobsters the previous week, the expedition to Red Sands Tower was a miserable failure.

We were delayed all the way down the River by fog and when it finally cleared enough to stop the mournful fog-horn and get into position near one of the giant struts, it was too late. The tide was running and the best we could do was to go down one of the Tower's legs in two foot visibility and collect a sack full of mussels.

It was interesting from the point of view that the seabed at 30 feet did really consist of red sand, well, rosy-coloured sand anyway. That dive also taught us the lesson that enthusiasm was not enough when diving in British waters. You simply have to be in the right spot at the right time from the point of view of tide or you are just wasting your air going in. There are, of course, exceptions to this rule where shelter from the tide can be found behind a large obstruction, but in this case the Tower's legs were just not big enough.

During the early spring I managed to get myself a boat in Britain too. Well, it was just about a boat. It cost me £20 and was an old clinker-built job that had seen better days, but with a small outboard on the back – a 3 h.p. Johnson – it did enable us to move about in the immediate area of Bognor Yacht Club.

You could hardly call it intrepid or vastly rewarding diving but, from the point of view of visibility after the two winter dives it was paradise.

Robin Messent, Mike Todd, Penny and I, tried diving on the reef and were amazed to find that despite its proximity to shore it contained a great deal more life than even we were prepared to expect. Robin tried some filming with his vast underwater camera case and though it was not very successful

Dominating the whole of the area around Aiguablava is Cap Bagur. This is the view when returning from a dive in the Place of the Gorgonias near Sa Tuna. Penny is sunbathing as usual on the engine hatch. The petrol tank is inside the wooden box on her right. (*See* Chapter Fourteen)

Spiny lobster at the entrance to his hole on Lobster Rock off the Costa Brava coast of Spain. Depth 40 ft. (*See* Chapter Fourteen)

John Messent with a spearfishing trophy — a 14 lb bass which he speared off Bognor, Sussex. (*See* Chapter Thirteen)

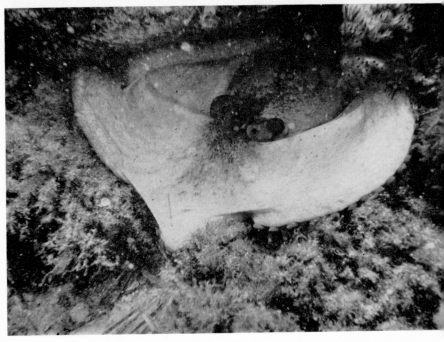

White with fear. An octopus often reacts this way to the first approach of a diver. Note the suckers exposed on the tentacle on the right. Picture taken at a depth of 35 feet in Vigueta Bay, near San Feliu de Guixols

This ugly red scorpion fish is just one of many on Lobster Rock near Aiguablava, Spain. His sting can produce agonising pain. (*See* Chapter Fourteen)

we felt it proved it could be done. Often with this sort of diving the onlooker sees more of the game than the photographer. It was the same in this case.

Robin was very preoccupied with the controls on his camera on one dive outside the reef. I hung in the water some feet away from him waiting while he fiddled. Suddenly to my surprise I saw that I was not the only one who was watching Robin's performance.

A great long garfish was also watching. With his tail curled up under his snake-like body like a great question mark he hung just to the right of Robin's head and seemed to be intent on peering into his face-mask. A bout of bubbles from the demand valve on the diver's neck did nothing to disturb him. He kept edging his pointed beak round towards Robin's face until I was sure that the two would soon be face to face. But Robin never saw him and finally, satisfied with the camera, flipped up his fins and headed downwards. The garfish obviously considered this the height of bad manners and left in a hurry.

Robin had good reason for not seeing this fish, but divers who insist on pushing into the depths suffer from 'rapture of the depth gauge' (just seeing how deep they can go) and miss seeing most of what goes on in the sea.

However, it is also true that there are divers who see a great deal on their dives and those who see little. The art of seeing things – fish and animal life in general – seems to depend to a large extent on the diver's temperament and experience. After a great deal of diving you do tend to notice things that are out of place – a flick of movement among weed, a colour just slightly different from the surroundings – but experience alone will not make you see things.

It is in many ways like a countryman and a town-dweller walking through a wood. The untrained eye will look hard but see nothing whereas the man who is used to seeing creatures in the trees and undergrowth will spot them almost at once. Some people though will never see.

I have often been amazed at the things other divers notice and point out to me long before I see them myself. Yet I find it difficult to understand or forgive a diver who after years of diving cannot identify even the commonest of fish which he sees underwater. These people do not seem to want to learn about the ways of the things they see under the sea – and I wonder sometimes why they dive at all.

Mind you, seeing something and relating it to what it really is can be a funny business underwater. A particular incident which illustrates this came that very summer when we went to Spain and took complete charge of *Penelope*.

Being in charge of a boat is a completely different thing from being a passenger in someone else's boat. I find the first situation a matter for concern and vigilance and the second a happy-go-lucky experience. My wife, Penny, thinks I am probably a born worrier, but I do find the winds of the Mediterranean a worry and am not ashamed to say so. It is easy when lying on a sun-soaked beach to raise your head and glance out at sea and say how calm it is. It is another matter to be out in a boat some distance off shore and to feel a wind start – a wind that can lick the sea into a turmoil in a matter of minutes.

Penny says I should never have talked to the fisherman of the Costa Brava because they are full, as fishermen the world over are inclined to be, of dire prophecies. I counter this by saying that these are the men who know the sea there and it is better to run for shelter ten minutes early than ten minutes late. So I worry too much and I think she worries too little. A typical married stalemate situation.

For those who care to share my worries about the wind – have you ever noticed how the wind upsets some people and not others? – here is a list of the winds you are likely to encounter on the Costa Brava reading from north to east to south to west.

The really unpleasant north wind is the Tramontana, then comes the Gargal, the Llevant, the Xaloc, the Migjorn, the Garbi, the Ponent, and the Mestral. And in my opinion you can't trust any of them!

The day I am writing about – the day when seeing was not really believing – came when, with Robin and Penny diving too, I saw a millstone jammed in a cleft of a shallow reef in Vigueta Bay just round the point of St Elmo near the harbour of San Feliu.

The day was one when there really could be no worry about

wind. It was flat calm and still. I saw this millstone, and it looked like a stone motor-tyre upright in the cleft. And I saw it and passed on. I didn't mention it until we were having drinks that evening. Why this was I can't tell you. I saw it and I said to myself : 'That's a Roman millstone' and I did nothing about it and went on with the dive. Mind you, I wasn't seeing things. It was there and we went back with the *Penelope* and hauled it out the next day.

I took the millstone back to England and had it dated as near as it could be. There was some suggestion that this was the millstone which had been used in an attempt to drown Saint Feliu when they were martyring him at the beginning of the 4th century. So I took the millstone back to San Feliu and handed it to the mayor, and it is there for you to see in the town museum. If you are interested in the story of that millstone it is all written down elsewhere.*

The range of our diving was now extended and Robin went filming mad. Everywhere we went his big brass underwater camera case would go with him and the huge cork float that was needed to keep him and the camera from plunging to the bottom in a crumpled heap. He was a familiar sight to me, you could always tell where he was. Floating along majestically above some reef of black rocks like a giant fish would come the light brown edges of the cork float and you knew that Robin was just the other side.

During this holiday a rock on the chart of the area caught our attention. It was in a direct line between Palamos and San Feliu and seemed a likely place to find an ancient wreck.

I asked Francisco about it. 'You mean La Llosa,' he said, 'there have been many wrecks there. It is a very dangerous place.' That was enough to send us off in search of it. The danger was that we would end up on it ourselves. But on a calm day we should be all right. Robin insisted that the time to go was very early in the morning. Then, he argued rightly, we could be sure of a calm sea.

So we set off very early. We had no trouble finding it for a little group of fishing boats were already clustered around it. I must say it was a diabolical trap for the unwary sailor. If you cleared the rocks round San Feliu and then set a direct

* *The Second Underwater Book* (Pelham Books).

course for the port of Palamos you were almost bound to hit it.

I can't say that I found the water appetising at that time in the morning, but once in, the Llosa provided a fascinating sight. It was like a solitary mountain soaring up from a flattish plain. And it's black fangs came to within two feet of the surface. It was correctly marked on the chart with a small black cross in a dotted ring – 'a rock with six feet or less water over it at chart datum . . .' – but failure to study the Admiralty chart of the area with care before setting sail across the bay to Palamost might well lead to shipwreck.

There was deep water all around the Llosa, but that hadn't saved a variety of ships through the ages. As I finned slowly down the sides of the rock mountain, the evidence of the deaths of those unlucky ships was clear to see. The lower slopes were spattered with wreckage and in the ravines and hummocks of sand around the actual base of the rock there was more. A large rusty winch indicated a ship of some size and sheets of iron or steel plating showed that it was not only small fishing boats or pleasure craft that had been the Llosa's victims.

I fanned away the sand near some of the wreckage and found evidence of the death of a ship of long ago. Laid out in rows as they must have been in the planking before that rotted away and disappeared were stout bronze nails with arrow-head points to stop them pulling out. (I thought these were dated to very ancient times, but further investigations indicated a possible use of such nails at much later dates.)

The depth here was 65 feet and though the sun was now well up it seemed a gloomy place. Locals have told me that pieces of amphora have been found around the rock and they say too that some visiting divers made themselves new weight belts from an old lead anchor stock they found there. I don't know if this is true. I doubt it.

I doubt it because visiting divers are hardly likely to have the facilities to melt down such a thing in their hotels or camp sites. And also because though such a thing might well end up as a souvenir in tourist divers' hands, they are less likely to destroy it than some less well-off fisherman who hauled it up in his nets. Certainly though, I do not doubt that ancient anchor stocks have been thoughtlessly destroyed in hundreds over the years for their lead.

But around the Llosa I found no evidence of such ancient souvenirs. As we finished the dive, Robin climbed out of the water and stood on the top. It was an amazing sight and one that I wish I had recorded with my camera. The water came

MAP 2. When we wanted to dive we usually turned down the coast after leaving the harbour of San Feliu and headed past Bosch Pt. to Canet Cove or even further on towards Tossa. If we headed north we were aiming for La Llosa, a treacherous rock which claimed many ships over the centuries.

up to his knees and there he stood as though walking on the water half-a-mile out to sea.

Though the Llosa can be easily avoided if you know it is there and the sea is calm, to pick it out in a rough or even choppy sea would be another matter. I was so impressed with what a hazard to shipping it was – while we were there a big speedboat 'shot us up' and despite our frantic signals missed the top of the rock by a mere foot or so – that I asked Francisco why they didn't do something about it.

'Do something?' he asked in return.

'Yes, blow the top off it with explosives.'

'What for? Everyone knows it is there.'

And that was that. But everyone didn't know it was there and each year or so another tourist yacht or speedboat would strike it and sink and the local divers would salvage what they could for the owners. Finally in 1970, however, they did do something about it.

Luis Villa, who is one of the most famous divers of the Costa Brava – his boat leaves San Feliu practically every day in the summer laden with tourist divers who get extremely good value for money – was told to blow the top off the Llosa. As would be expected from a professional like Villa, the job was done extremely well and the big bang was covered by Spanish television and newspapers as a major news event. Now at long last it looks as though the Llosa has claimed its last victim.

'H.M.S. *Penelope*' (as Francisco now called our boat) proved to be the making of our holidays and we roamed the seas around San Feliu finding new places to dive on each mini-voyage.

As a result the amount of equipment that we needed to take with us on holidays abroad just grew and grew. I suppose all of it wasn't really necessary, but the aqualung bottles certainly took up a great deal of room and now there was gear for the boat. The Vanguard shooting brake coped easily with the extra load and though it had proved how tough it was, it was about to be put to the test again.

Spain was still our target for holidays and they always centred around San Feliu de Guixols. The town seemed to have everything we needed. Spanish friends, clear water, a compressor where we could pump up our bottles, good hotels and best of all a rate of exchange that made the millionaire life possible compared with the steep price rises that took place in France.

The children, Kevin and Joanna, enjoyed the camping that

we did in France on the way down to Spain much more than I did. Camping to me was never anything but a makeshift and I'm not so sure that we saved all that much. Telling ourselves that we were saving vast sums of money just led to spending vast amounts on evening meals at good restaurants near the camping sites we visited.

But we also reckoned that camping made us get on with the journey more than if we had stayed at a hotel. Forced out of my tent – the children and Penny slept in comparative style in the Vanguard with a cover over it – by torrential rains I would happily motor for a hundred miles before breakfast.

On one occasion this was our undoing. We had put nearly 100 before breakfast miles on the clock when we passed through Morterelles-sur-Semme. As I accelerated out of the village some sort of disturbance caught my eye – some people from a green Austin A.30 appeared to be involved in a fight on the opposite side of the road. I slowed and then looked back at the road.

I was too late. The French driver ahead of me had seen the same scene and had braked to a halt in the middle of the Route Nationale. I had no chance of avoiding him and with a last desperate squeal of brakes the Vanguard piled into the back of the stationary Simca.

The person who goes into the back of another in France is, as in most other countries, automatically to blame. And, to be fair, I suppose I was. That didn't help matters as the shattered front of the Vanguard poured the contents of its radiator back down the hill into the village.

Fortunately neither the children nor Penny had been hurt though the luggage rack containing diving gear shot forward yards ahead of the crash and the bottles had forced the back seat down and cascaded luggage over the children in the back seat. Once we were over our shock – and had made sure that the French couple were unhurt – it looked as though our holiday was over. But I had reckoned without the tough Vanguard chassis and the skill of the French mechanics of Morterelles-sur-Semme.

Within two hours they had me back on the road with a welded up radiator and very little else of the front intact. It looked a fearful mess, but it still went. Hours late we limped into Gerona in Spain – only to have one of the front circular springs snap as we bounced towards San Feliu.

But we made it and the Spanish mechanics of the town then took over. They made a new spring by grinding another one down. They beat out the shattered front bodywork so well that on my return to London all I had to do was to have it re-sprayed. Years of improvisation – keeping their old cars on the road before new ones were freely available – has turned the Spaniard into a first-class car mechanic. In fact that improvised spring was so well done that it lasted the life of the car as well as meeting the strict check made on the car on my return.

So we had reached Spain once again. But the diving had changed over the years. It all happened so slowly that we really never noticed it at the time. Spearfishing had taken its toll of the popular areas and there was no longer a fish under every rock. What had once been quiet little coves or sandy beaches that sported only a few tourists and Spanish holiday families were now crowded with tourists from every country of Europe.

I am not saying that the rush of tourists to Spain was a bad thing. It was inevitable when we foreigners found that Spanish prices were the cheapest in Europe, with perhaps the exception of Yuglosavia. I'm sad about the fish, but not sorry for what tourism has done to the living standards of most ordinary Spaniards.

The money that we, the tourists, poured into the country has done more to bring Spain face to face with the 20th Century than anything else could have done.

Of course, we have brought them some bad things – the worst of civilisation always travels the quickest, but only the selfish will mourn the passing of the poor peasant who would serve you with anything that he had for a few pesetas.

By all means let us reminisce about the 'good old days' when you could 'buy a round of drinks for 20 people and still have change from ten bob', but don't let's forget what that cheapness meant in terms of hard work and little reward. Nobody has ruined Spain, unless by ruined you mean that prices have gone up.

Francisco was now diving again – cautiously. But he was diving. We went out with him in *Penelope* on this particular day even though the Garbi was kicking the sea up into quite a chop. On the way back to San Feliu Francisco suggested that we finish up the air in our bottles on a lonely rock. There seemed no particular reason to do so as we were on our way back to harbour for lunch. But Francisco seemed keen and when I asked him why he replied simply that he liked oysters.

We finned down through a small ravine and levelled off at about 45 feet. Though there was only one pinnacle showing on the surface, here it was clear there was a complex of rocks underwater rearing up from the sea bed and looking ghostly white with barnacled growth. The pale rocks stood out starkly against the dark blue of the deep water all around, but for the life of me I could not see any oysters.

Francisco started digging away at the white rocks with his diving knife and I came closer to watch. Our bubbles rose from the demand valves until looking up I could see two streams of white expired air moving upward in steady columns until they got near the surface. There the chop got hold of them and they swerved this way and that before merging with the surface.

Francisco saw me just watching and gesticulated at the rock surface with a get-on-with-it sign. Then I saw what we were after. A thin dark slit in the rock would close when tapped with Francisco's knife. If it failed to close he would abandon it and move on to another. I moved even closer and saw that the whole upper surface of the rock seemed to be covered with these dark slits and realised that I was looking at a large oyster colony.

In next to no time – we had practically no time with the little air that was left in the bottles – we had collected a whole bag full, though the proportion of oysters that didn't close when tapped, and so were presumably dead, was quite high.

I took a couple of dozen back to the Murla and we ate them immediately with Ramon and Josef Murla. Complete with lemon of course. Unfortunately, this excellent pre-lunch snack was to have dire results for Penny. She was violently ill later and it was the first idea that we had that she was allergic to oysters.

Two days before our holiday came to an end we took a land trip that was to make a complete change in our holiday and diving pattern. We went out to lunch on an exchange ticket. This system is still worked by certain hotels on the Costa Brava and simply means that if you go out for a drive you can go to any one of the listed hotels, produce your exchange ticket, and have lunch without further payment.

You pay for the lunch at your own hotel in your normal pension charge and I suppose some sort of settling up takes place with the tickets at the end of the season between the hoteliers themselves.

We took an exchange ticket for the Hotel Aigua Blava further north on the Costa Brava and, apart from the excellent lunch, we were overwhelmed with the beauty of the setting. On one side the great headland of Cap Bagur stretched rose-red out to sea. On the other Mut Point had fingers in the deep blue sea. In between the green pines the little bay of Aiguablava itself sparkled in the sun. The diving looked fabulous and on the spot Robin, Pauline, Penny and I decided to try and spend our next summer holiday there. The difficulty we soon found was getting into the hotel. There was what amounted to a waiting list even to be considered for a place.

A long chat in the hotel reception with a smiling sophisticated man who seemed at home in any language you cared to try – we settled on English – seemed to bring only slight hope of a place if we wrote early in January the following year.

That was our first meeting with Xiquet Sabater, hotelier, sentimentalist, businessman, expansionist, conservative, diplomat and Olympic swimmer.

It was clear to me then that we were talking to an extraordinary man, but it certainly wasn't clear that he was going to let us into his hotel the next summer. What we didn't know then was that Xiquet Sabater is Aiguablava. He had built the hotel up after the Spanish Civil War from a fisherman's house to the magnificent hotel it is today (his grandfather is said to have been the first man to call the coast the Costa Brava – the Rugged Coast) and could even then make his own choice from the potential guests clamouring to get in.

We left the hotel without a firm 'yes' or 'no'. Robin, Pauline and Penny rated our chances as pretty poor. But I was determined. The area looked unlikely to have been heavily dived and I wanted to stay there.

This didn't mean that San Feliu was not still fine for a holiday, but it was, I thought, time for a change. And there seemed no reason why we couldn't bring *Penelope* up the coast – it was only 15 miles by sea – and have the best of both worlds.

Chapter
Eleven

In the course of our work Peter Small and I met now and again. The British Sub-Aqua Club, which he and Oscar Gugen had founded was going from strength to strength. In September 1962 Peter married Mary Miles, daughter of aircraft designer Frederick Miles. The national newspapers made great play of the fact that they were to spend their honeymoon diving in the Mediterranean, but the real thing about this marriage from the point of view of those who knew them was that they were the storybook 'perfect match' and if ever a woman loved anyone Mary loved Peter.

That autumn soon after their return from honeymoon Peter rang me at the *Evening News*. He had, he said, something important to discuss with me – something that would make a great story for the paper.

We met, because we were both in Fleet Street, in the office restaurant on the sixth floor of Harmsworth House, the home of the *Evening News*. We sat, I remember, at a table in the autumn sunlight looking out over the nearby Temple. I offered him some wine, but he refused saying that he was in training. That word 'training' was the key to the whole subject he wanted to discuss with me.

The project that he unveiled then left me almost speechless. He was, he said, going to accompany Hannes Keller, the 28-year-old Swiss mathematician and deep sea diver to the seabed 1,000 feet down off the Californian coast in December that year.

Keller's experiments with breathing mixtures I knew a great deal about – he had already made several record dives – but the idea of Peter Small, though a wiry fellow, being fit enough to take part in such a venture worried me.

I said as much to Peter. 'I'm doing masses of training – swimming and running every day. I'll be all right,' he said dismissing my concern and went on to elaborate about the dive.

They would be lowered to the seabed in a diving bell. Once there the hatch in the floor would be opened and they would swim out to establish a new world record. 'After that,' said Peter, 'I'll be the expert on the subject . . . the journalist who knows about the deep sea.' To be fair that was, I know, the least of his interests in the dive – he believed with all his heart in the future of the exploration by man of the deep sea. He believed that with the 1,000 feet depth bogey beaten, all the continental shelves of the world could be opened up to men, and he wanted to be there in the forefront of that new world.

I felt nothing but apprehension about the whole thing. Perhaps I was imagining how I would feel down there. But Peter was quite firm. He was a brave man.

Then we came to the reason for the meeting. He wanted to know if the *Evening News* would be prepared to pay for his exclusive reports on the 1,000 feet dive. As a journalist he would not fail to give us fine material – there was no doubt in my mind about that. But the price was high and we never did come to an agreement.

Peter went ahead – his fitness was obviously not in doubt for he took part with success in simulated dives to the 1,000 foot depth – and on the 4th December 1962 the dive started off Catalina Island, California. Within hours John Gold, who was then the *Evening News* New York Correspondent and is now Editor, started dictating over the telephone to London : 'Two British frogmen died today during an attempt to break the world's deep-diving record.

'They were Peter Small, a 35-year-old journalist of Duke Street, Westminster, who had been married less than three months, and Christopher Whittaker, a 19-year-old student of Cherry Hill Farm, Coleshill, Bucks.

'Small had been lowered in a diving bell 1,000 feet into the dark depths of the Pacific off the Californian coast where the pressure is 30 times that on the surface.

'With him was the ace Swiss diver Hannes Keller.

'Something went wrong on the sea floor. As the diving bell was hurriedly being raised Whittaker and another man dived to the rescue.

'At 200 feet Whittaker struggled to close a jammed hatch

on the diving bell. He returned to the surface to fetch a knife.

'With blood pouring from his nostrils he was ordered out of the water. But he ignored it, grabbed the knife and dived again. His bravery cost him his life. Watchers on the surface never saw him again. Ships and planes searched for him in vain.

'When the diving bell was hauled alongside its escort ship Small was found inside unconscious. Keller too was suffering from lack of oxygen.

'Both men were rushed to Long Beach Naval Hospital. Small died there. At his bedside was his 23-year-old bride, Mary . . .'

The report went on. I read it with horror. The project that Peter had told me about so calmly that sunny autumn day had cost two lives, one of them his own.

Keller recovered completely and went on with his experiments. A post mortem on Peter showed that he had died from the bends – from the expansion of nitrogen bubbles in his bloodstream. But Mary Small held up bravely saying that despite Peter's death she felt the deep diving experiments should go on.

Back in London she seemed to be taking her loss well. Perhaps too well but those who talked with her could not have realised that her heart was broken and she had no wish to go on living. But she told us that she wanted to go on promoting the work that Peter had begun.

On the 12th of February, 1963, I was News Editor of the *Evening News* when I was told there was a personal call for me. The caller told me in a few words that Mary had been found dead in their gas-filled flat with photographs of Peter around her.

It was a news story. A news story that the *Evening News* faithfully told, but it was one that I hoped I would never have to write.

I knew the area where Peter Small had died, not well, but I knew it. This had come about because the year before the *Evening News* had sent me on a U.S. State Department trip to report on the American radar Early Warning System. We had flown to Greenland where I met some divers who thought nothing of cutting a hole in the frozen sea and diving through it (I suspect to relieve the boredom of an enforced stay in the U.S. base at Thule.) We then moved on to Point Barrow in the Arctic where only a maniac would think of diving at all and had finally after a short stay in Alaska reached the full comforts of civilisation at Los Angeles.

It was there, not far from the great seaquarium of Marineland where I would like to believe that only time stopped me from taking up an invitation to join the diver who was feeding the sharks underwater, that I had some idea of how popular the sport of skin diving is in California. As we looked down from the clifftops on to the beach chosen – I think by 'Skin Diver' magazine – for a skin divers' meet, the whole stony beach appeared to be crawling with seals. The 'seals' turned into skin divers in black neoprene wet suits when we reached sea level. I was a bit put off by the suits. Surely this was the Pacific? I had borrowed only enough gear to dive, not a suit to keep me warm. But an introduction to 'Miss Underwater Temptress' and 'Miss Skin Diver' at a booth on the beach sent me scurrying glowing, to the water.

The visibility was good, but the Pacific was freezing and everywhere I looked there were black-suited bodies all around me. It was hardly the most auspicious introduction to diving in the Pacific and I was really quite glad to get out of the water. But it did give me some idea of the number of people concerned with skin diving in the U.S.A. compared with our then happy few back in Britain.

Our 'home' diving was beginning now to be divided between British waters and Spanish. But not divided equally. Our Mediterranean diving consisted of one spurt of three weeks, diving every day, and our ventures into British waters were spread out from April to October each year, diving at every suitable week-end.

The extraordinary thing was that I was beginning to find myself less fearful of Britain's lower visibility and greener waters that I was when in the blue, and in visibility in excess of 100 feet which we often encountered in Spain. If I had indeed suffered from a touch of claustrophobia in that Spanish cave then this seemed to be a complete contradiction. Surely I would have been unhappier in waters where the visibility was often down to a few feet and sometimes only inches than in the wide open full visibility waters off the coast of the Costa Brava?

I began to doubt that I had indeed suffered from claustrophobia and what I was inclined to suffer from was, in reality, pure fear.

For one reason or another – the main one being that 'Polly' Messent was now pregnant with what later turned out to be Peter – we reversed the usual order of holidays the year after we took charge of our boat *Penelope*.

Instead of going diving in Britain and then in the middle of the season taking our holiday abroad, this year we went to Spain at the end of April – to the Aigua Blava Hotel. I'm sure that letting us in at this time solved a 'great' problem for Xiquet Sabater. He had no difficulty in giving us rooms in his hotel at that time of the year and he also stopped me from deluging him with letters requesting rooms at the height of the season.

It was our first visit to Spain in the spring and I'm sure that those who also only go in the summer don't realise what they are missing. The days were hot and the nights cold enough for a fire to crackle happily in the bar. The sea, as I found out in a foolish unsuited moment, was freezing, but this worried us not at all because we simply slipped into full wet suits.

On the first night at the hotel we walked out on to the terrace by the pine trees and in the light of the moon the whole hillside seemed to be full of bird song. Stupidly I commented on this to Penny openly in the bar when we came inside. It was some ridiculous remark about birds singing at night.

'Young man,' said a voice which I tracked down to a white-haired lady sitting at one of the little tables, 'those are nightingales and the other call you can hear is a migrating owl...' I felt a complete fool, but that woman turned out to be a distinguished ornithologist who reeled off information about the migrating habits of birds that we were likely to see in Spain at that time of year. She was, as are all experts who really know their subject and are not out to impress, absolutely fascinating about winged life.

The next problem was how to get *Penelope* up the coast from San Feliu. Robin and I with all the brashness of inexperience worked out that *Penelope* did about 5 knots. The distance by sea as the seagull flies was about 15 miles. Therefore the sea trip should take us about three hours. We would

144

start early from San Feliu – leaving one of our cars there to be picked up later – and come up the coast in grand style. It was going to be a doddle.

But it wasn't. Everything worked out to plan until we reached the Palamos Shoal just outside the big harbour there. We were doing jolly well and estimated that we might clip ten minutes off our estimate of three hours.

We had reckoned without the winds of the Mediterranean. By the time we had rounded Molino Point and started heading up the coast towards Calella and Llafranch we were in seas that began to be quite frightening.

We thought at first that we were butting into an ordinary head wind, but now we know that we were trying to buck a tramontana. Not a full tramontana, which howls down from the north, but the beginning of one. When a wave broke over the bow and sloshed down the broad sill at the bulwarks and finally emptied itself into the sea behind us, I looked questioningly at Robin. 'The boat was built for these seas,' he shouted, but there seemed a singular lack of conviction in his voice.

From then on as we rose and fell, butted and rolled through the seas, I was, and I found out later that Robin was too, looking for likely spots to swim ashore and to hell with the boat.

I think the rounding of Cape St Sebastian was the worst moment. We were cold, we were soaked and giant rollers lifted us 20 feet up and then we began the sickening run down into the trough. *Penelope* behaved very well, but gallons of water poured over the engine hatch and our feet were now permanently in water sloshing about in bilges.

At that moment I would willingly have abandoned the whole trip and turned in for shore, but there was no way out there. A wall of white foam marked the shoreline at the foot of the cliffs and I debated with myself whether to turn back.

The trouble was that turning would be more hazardous than pushing on. Every now and then it would seem to me that the engine was faltering. In reality, of course, it kept thumping away as Spanish fishing boat engines usually do. Even so I think we would have turned back if it were not for the sudden appearance of a Spanish fisherman. It was ridiculous. There we were fearing for our lives and suddenly high above us was a Spaniard in what one can only describe as a rowing boat, sculling with one oar and pulling up a lobster pot with the other. He was a most reassuring sight even if he was a difficult man to have a conversation with – one moment he was right above us, the next he was down in a trough several feet of green water below.

I felt the need to communicate. 'Aiguablava?' I screamed at him in what I hoped was a question. 'Donde?' he shrieked back. 'Aiguablava.' 'Aiguablava si,' his words were whipped back by the wind, 'pero Sa Tuna no.' I took this to mean that we were all right to get into Aiguablava, but if we were heading for the little creek of Sa Tuna we would never make it.

We waved an acknowledgement and he went on smiling and hauling on the rope to the pot. He had no free arm to acknowledge, but the mere sight of him was comforting.

So we crept on up the coast. We had throttled the engine back – any attempt at full throttle would we were sure have merely resulted in a headlong dive to the seabed. By the time we reached the level of the popular resort of Tamariu we agreed without any argument to turn in and seek shelter for a while and then consider whether we should go on. At any rate it was obviously advisable to refuel in some sheltered bay.

How we laugh now about our arrival in Tamariu. But at the time it was anything but funny. Once inside the shelter of the headland the water became something more like the Mediterranean that is shown on every travel poster. We, however, were not in the least like the bronzed jolly sailors on those same posters. Both of us had every article of clothing around us that we could lay our hands on. Both of us wore lifejackets. We were so cold that we might have been battling a Bognor gale. As we came into the little jetty on the right hand side of the bay as you enter from the sea, rows of sunbathers on the little beach sat up row by row and looked at us in amazement.

To them of course the Mediterranean was flat calm in their sheltered haven. Just looking out from their prone position soaking up the sun they had no idea of the hellish conditions out at sea. Indeed they would not have believed it if you had told them.

Robin and I felt a bit idiotic all wrapped up as we were. But worse was to come. We went into the first of the little beach-front bars that are a feature of Tamariu and ordered brandies. We were both shaking with cold. The woman behind the bar poured our brandies into minute glasses that would have been more suitable for some porcelain tea-party. Robin and I looked at them. We tried to lift them and the brandy slopped out. Finally we hit on the only solution – leave the glass on the bar and get our heads down to them. I looked at the woman hesitantly. She almost read my thoughts. 'It's quite all right,' she said, 'we get a lot of people like that.' The inference was obvious.

Several brandies later Robin and I were convinced that the sea could not have been as rough as we had imagined and we set off again. We found out. Once we had rounded the shelter of Tamariu Point the sea hit us again, but we finally made it to Aiguablava Bay where Polly and Penny were sunbathing and wondering why we were so late. I don't know if they ever believed us.

The next day the baby tramantana had blown itself out, though it had not forgotten – and was to return in adult guise a few days later.

We dived every day that it was possible – in full suits to keep warm – and I began to use the first underwater 35 m.m. camera, a Calypsophot, that I had ever owned. The pictures that I took then were to cement my tinkerings with underwater photography into a full-blown passion.

The diving at Aiguablava proved to be all that we had hoped. Though one or two spearfishermen did occasionally work out along Cap Bagur, in general the waters had been undisturbed by large numbers of divers.

Though I had taken pictures with various cameras during earlier diving this was the first chance I really had of using the waterproof 35 m.m. cameras which are now quite normal equipment for underwater photographers.

Like so much underwater apparatus the pioneers in this field were the French and the Calypsophot which was the first, to be followed by the Japanese Nikonos, are just the same to look at as any other small camera. In fact you can still cause some photographers to have something approaching a heart attack when you calmly wash the salt water off your camera by holding it under the nearest freshwater tap.

All the controls work through seals and two big O-ring seals make sure that the lens fitting and the top of the camera, which you lift out to put in more film, are completely watertight. The manufacturers say that these cameras can be used quite safely down to 160 feet and the greater the pressure of water on them up to that depth the tighter the seal. In fact, friends have taken cameras of this type deeper than 160 feet with no harm coming to them.

I took my Calypsophot on all ten dives we made that year in and around Aiguablava Bay – the return of the tramontana in full force accounts for the fact that there were not more dives – and was delighted with the results. If they were not award-winning shots at any rate they pleased me.

And they certainly pleased me more than the results I got on our return to week-end diving at Bognor, but then I had still to learn how to cope with photography in low visibility waters.

Looking in my diving log-book I see that the year we first went to Aiguablava seemed a good one for new diving spots. Penny and I made a habit of going at least once a week to Downham Baths – or Ladywell Baths, Lewisham – when the Bromley Branch, our branch, of the British Sub-Aqua Club rented the pool for the evening for training purposes.

On these evenings at the pool and in the pub afterwards there was of course a great deal of diving gossip. Branch members would come back from holiday or from some diving trip and express themselves in forthright terms about the conditions they had encountered. One small group seemed to have found the perfect place – if you were to believe everything they said about it. The word 'Manacles' occurred in practically every sentence they spoke.

The Manacles it seemed were *the* spot to dive. They had everything – clear water, big fish, wrecks . . . the advantages of the place seemed endless. So Penny and I decided to go and have a look.

First of all let us establish what we are talking about. The Manacles are a group of rocks with a savage reputation just off the Lizard in Cornwall. The nearest place to them is the little village of Porthoustock with its beach of grey stones that

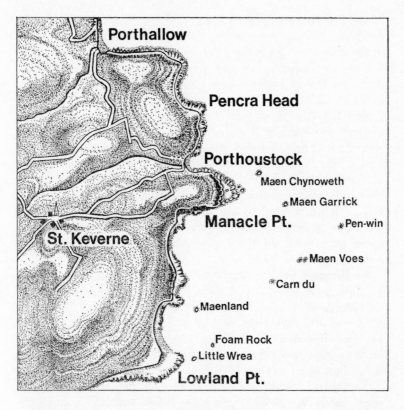

MAP 3. The Manacles off the coast of Cornwall have a bloody reputation. These rocks have claimed many large ships and over a hundred people have died there in a single night. Today's divers find not only the graves of known wrecks, but sometimes the remains of ships, which were sunk without trace or record.

has been built up over the years as a result of the quarrying for granite chips that has gone on in the immediate vicinity.

On either side of the little bay are great quarry buildings and at one time the ships used to come right in under shoots down which the stone would pour into the hold. That doesn't happen very often there now as the beach has built up so much that most of the shoots jut out over water only a few feet deep.

Porthoustock (Prowstock the locals call it) Beach is not

in itself a beautiful place – it has a sombre look even in bright sunlight – but the surrounding countryside and coastline is some of the most beautiful in the world.

Bromley Branch members who first discovered the diving there, as far as London divers are concerned, were fortunate in their first contact.

Bernard Rogers, a local farmer, is a bull of a man with massive shoulders well suited to the hard work of farming – and the carrying of heavy diving equipment from spot to spot. But, unlike most bulls, he is highly intelligent. He owned a boat at Porthoustock and did a deal of fishing for the big pollack, bass and mackerel that teem in Cornish waters. Not content with this he wanted to see under the water and what fishes were like at home. Both he and his ever-cheery wife, Colleen, could swim well on the surface. But Bernard wanted to see more.

So Bromley Branch taught him to dive. In exchange he and his fishermen friends used their boats and local knowledge to provide good diving. In fact there grew up between the fishermen and the divers the sort of relationship that should exist between the two groups. (It culminated recently in a full-scale salvage operation to recover a fishing boat that had gone down in a storm on the Manacles).

Penny and I and the children were late arriving on the diving scene there. We should have gone before we did. A lot of the pioneering work had already been done. Roy Davis, a member of Bromley Branch, who now lives in Cornwall and is one of the West Country's most expert divers, and Bernard Rogers had done a good deal of research on wrecks in the vicinity and had positions for some of them.

Our first visit then was at the beginning of September and the warm welcome from Colleen and Bernard was very cheering. I can't say that I found my first sight of the Manacles the same.

Perhaps I had been conditioned by reading the preliminary research done by people like Alan Smith of Bromley Branch into the history of the Manacles and the shipwrecks on them. They have a bloody record and we only know of losses that are written down. What their toll was before records were fully kept it is impossible to say. Ships were frailer then and as the Manacles have ripped the bottom out of modern ships, they would have had little difficulty with ancient craft.

Standing on the cliff top at Manacle Point not far from Bernard's farm and looking out over a grey sea it was easy to see why the Manacles have earned their place in the history of shipwrecks. Out, well out from the shore, almost a mile in fact, there are only a few signs of the trap that lies below the surface. Shark's Fin shows close in. Further out so does Maen Chynoweth. And Maen Garrick. And Maen Voes and Carn Du. But the real secret of the Manacles (a corruption of Maen Eglos, the Cornish for Church Rocks) is that there is far more underwater than ever shows above.

Rocks rear up from the seabed at 140 or 150 feet to within ten feet or less of the surface. And this is why now that the Manacles are extensively dived sometimes the divers find wreckage for which there is no record, no explanation. They are finning over a ship that died in the night. Over a hundred people have been known to die on the Manacles in a single shipwreck, and perhaps the most famous of them all is the *Mohegan*.

The *Mohegan* hit the Manacles on Friday, October 14th, 1898 – and she hit them at almost full speed. It is an amazing story. This was no tramp butting about the world's oceans in search of a living; this was a new passenger liner headed for New York. But the course they set was such that if the Manacles had not claimed her she would have hit the Lizard itself!

She was 482 feet long, 52 feet wide and 34 feet 6 inches deep and her tonnage was 8,500. And when she hit the Manacles 106 people drowned. For the full story you must turn, elsewhere,* but as I stood looking out at the Manacles it was easy to visualise that night.

Far out the Manacles Bell tolled gloomy warnings of the dangers of the reef. It is an awe-inspiring place. And so was my first sight of the Manacles underwater.

Where was all the clear water they raved about? Penny and I went down the anchor rope to 70 feet and found ourselves in a slightly luminescent brown haze with a maximum visibility of ten feet. This was on one of the Manacle Rocks called

* *The Wreck Hunters* (Harrap).

151

Pen Win. It was terribly disappointing and the surface was pretty off-putting too.

A big swell made the sea boil in white foam around those rocks that broke the surface. What I can only describe as 'pits' opened in the surface of the sea and then filled up with horrible gurgling noises. It seemed altogether an inhospitable place and not at all the diving spot that we had been led to expect. My uneasiness was not helped by the fact that with two more divers down, the anchor rope on Bernard's boat parted silently and frayed edges showed the cutting power of one unseen portion of the Manacles.

However, things perked up the next day. This time we dived – with Malcolm Todd who had been one of the Manacles pioneers – on Shark's Fin Rock to look for sea-urchins.

At that time the great big sea-urchins of Western waters were a comparative rarity on shore. Now every souvenir shop in the West Country has the shells minus the prickles on sale – usually made up into little lamps.

But then the sea-urchin industry had scarcely started and we took only those that we wanted to decorate our own homes. At first sight – and the visibility had improved – there was no sign of sea-urchins at all when we dived on Shark's Fin. The bottom was a waving mass of laminaria weed and I looked around in vain for the urchins which one and all had assured me could be as big as a football when viewed underwater.

'Mike' Todd showed us where they were when he went head first into the kelp parting it before him with both hands. He emerged with a great purple football of spikes and pointed down into the kelp. With some hesitation we did the same. There was quite a space under the weed carpet and by clinging on to the weed's holdfasts it was possible to move around in the forest. My first sight of a sea-urchin was of a ghostly white glow a few feet to my right. On a closer approach it turned into a beautiful pinky-purple globe and though that first one seemed huge you kept on seeing bigger and bigger ones, discarding the smaller ones, which tumbled back into safety as you let them go.

The urchins were not the only inhabitants of that underweed world. Big spidercrabs clung motionless to the weed in the green water and did nothing to hinder your picking them up – in fact they made it easier by contracting their great long spiders legs up underneath them so that you were left holding a tight compact mass of crab across the back. We let the spider-crabs go after posing them for photographs. We were not on a spider-crab collecting foray or we would have kept them for the pot. Few people seem to realise that there is plenty of good meat in one of these creatures and connoisseurs of crab say that it is sweeter than the flesh of the usual edible ones.

The next day – our last, for we had only a long week-end to spare, I made my first wreck dive on the Manacles. Target was the liner *Mohegan* – the largest wreck on the rocks.

In 1961, Roy Davis and Bernard Rogers had located the wreckage. They had used an aquaplane, the simple device that I had used in Spain, to find her. Out of the gloom in about 60 feet of water the ship's great boilers had loomed up out of the murk. The aquaplane was abandoned to float to the surface. The wreck of the *Mohegan* was found close to the rock that the local fishermen call the Voices.

The *Mohegan*'s bow is in 50 feet of water and her stern in 70 depending on the tide. My depth gauge showed 70 feet as I slid down the anchor rope and saw the line continuing through some rusting plating in which the anchor had smashed a hole. To my right what had obviously been the guide-rail around some part of the lost ship sagged away into the grey-white, almost luminous fog of 20 feet of visibility. Roy Davis, who dived with me, finned over the broken plating and slid down and out of sight. I felt fear, but not the same kind of fear that had come to me 100 feet down in Spain. This was a fear of losing my sense of direction and wandering away from the safety of the line back to the surface. So I finned around in the immediate vicinity of the anchor rope.

It was I found all a little bit too much for bold fearless exploration. The Voices . . . The Manacles . . . the *Mohegan* . . . here where I was finning were the remains that had cost 106 people their lives. Yet it wasn't gloomy down there. Far from it. It was almost bright with the sea a pale grey all around me.

I took a little courage and started studying my surroundings more carefully. Was there some souvenir that I could take back to the daylight of this jumbled wreckage beneath the sea? I remembered Bernard Rogers words before I dived – 'she looks like a Nissen hut that an elephant has sat on'. He was right. There was really no romance in it. I was finning over a jumble of meaningless wreckage. No doubt elsewhere the wreckage of the *Mohegan* takes shape and form and one can visualise the great ship that she was. But now I had no time.

My pressure gauge was in the red. I waited as long as I could and as Roy Davis appeared from out of the mist I signalled that I was going up and up I went. Somewhere only a short distance below me I could tell, by the jerking of the line, he was coming up too.

I surfaced empty handed. No souvenir from the sea. But I had captured something of the pull that the Manacles have for the divers. And I wanted to see more.

That night sitting before a roaring fire in the home of Mrs Rodgers (no relation to Bernard Rogers) and attempting to do justice to her idea of a small meal – the Cornish really are the great eaters of the world – I tried to analyse the fascination that I already felt about that part of Cornwall.

It wasn't just the diving, which quite frankly I thought pretty dangerous, though later years were to calm my fears. It wasn't just the warm content of Bernard Rogers farmhouse, though that of course had a lot to do with it. It wasn't the climate, though one high summer in Cornwall was to rival later the heat of Spain.

It had though, a great deal to do with the feeling of awe that one gets from standing on a Cornish cliff and looking down at the sea. The sense of history that you find in just a casual walk through St Keverne Churchyard only a short distance from the Manacles and Porthoustock Beach. And the sense of peace that comes from strolling anywhere on the Lizard.

We left Cornwall the next morning, but though the children were unhappy to leave the fields and the horses, I wasn't so upset. I knew we would be coming back.

It was late in the season now and we were to have only one more dive of interest that year. This was on Spires Mark off Bognor. It was late in the season, but the sea went glassy calm – the sort of sea that my old wreck of a boat was really suited for. Penny, Robin Messent and I drift dived following the boat by sight for the visibility was exceptional and clear from seabed to surface.

We moved slowly over a sand and gravel bottom with a few low outcrops of dark rock each with its clump of weed firmly attached. We saw pollack, pouting and more than one bass. But Penny made the best find of all. She picked up an old anchor. It was old but still serviceable even if the pattern went out of production in the late 1800's and though its getting a bit thin we still use it as a standby to this day.

Chapter
Twelve

It is usually true to say that you are safer underwater than you are on the surface. Certainly this thought is put into most divers' heads during training to stress that the real moment of danger is often the moment of surfacing.

It is then that the diver is most vulnerable. And it is true that there is a moment on just surfacing when all orientation is lost. Then the diver is inclined to spin in the water looking wildly around him for something – usually the diving boat – from which he can get his bearings. It is at this moment that he stands in real danger of being run down by surface traffic. One of my spearfishing friends was killed that way in Italy.

In fact, in a rough sea, the diver is safer underwater than on the surface because as a general rule the disturbance created by waves underwater is exactly the same depth as the height of the waves above the surface. In other words it would take a 60-foot wave to create a disturbance 60 feet down. I cannot imagine a diver being out in such conditions, but if such a thing did occur and a tidal wave of some height were to sweep down on a diving boat, in theory everyone should don diving gear and make a rapid descent to the safety of the bottom.

Having been out in some rough conditions I have the same respect for the sea as do the fishermen. On second thoughts that is not true. I have a respect and a fear of the sea while most fishermen I know only have the respect.

Yet only a fool would dive when he didn't want to. The fact that he might be called 'chicken' should never drive a diver into the water. Diving is something to be done in a state of calm, not of stretched, nerves – and after my earlier experiences I certainly know that to be true.

I have only to the best of my knowledge jibbed at a dive once – and that was on the Manacles in a calm sea and ideal diving conditions. Call me 'chicken' on this occasion and I'll agree.

The odd thing about this dive was that the depth was nothing to worry about. But I think my reason for not diving was pretty good. We had gone out in Bernard Roger's boat with Roy Davis, who was bent on collecting specimens for his salt-water aquarium. We anchored in a lapping sea with only 30 feet of water under the keel. Roy dived and set about his specimen collecting. Penny and I were almost completely kitted up when I heard Bernard's son, Keith, say to his father: 'That's a big one, Dad.' I looked up from fastening the quick-release on my weight-belt and saw a black rock close to the diving boat.

I looked down again at the release which was being particularly obstinate and then looked up again. The 'rock' was moving – and another 'rock' was following it some 15 feet behind. The second 'rock' was a great black fin and on a retake so was the first. I knew immediately what it was. A great basking shark was moving along close to the boat. Bernard had told me that at certain times in the year the basking sharks came into Porthoustock Bay and were quite harmless.

I stopped trying to get into my gear and grabbed for the camera – the results I'm sorry to say were disappointing as the wide-angle underwater lens made the shark's fins look so far away. Penny and I stared at the fins until they disappeared under the surface. As they did so Roy Davis climbed out of the water with a bulging specimen net. 'Aren't you going in?' he asked as the water dripped down from his pushed-up mask. 'No,' I replied firmly – 'we are not.'

'Go on,' said Bernard, 'it won't hurt you . . .' 'Why don't you go in then?' I countered. 'I,' said Bernard with a wide grin, 'have got a wife and kids to think of.'

Other suggestions that I should dive with Penny met with my blank refusal. My resolve was strengthened by Roy saying that the water was full of plankton and the visibility was bad.

This proliferation of plankton was, of course the reason the basking shark was so close inshore. He or she was feeding. So Bernard took us back even closer inshore for a dive. But neither Penny nor I enjoyed it. The water was like a green soup with thousands of little yellow dots in every foot – and I kept on expecting a great head to push through the murk and the basking shark to be upon us. I fired off every flash-bulb I had at sea-urchins and anything else that would make a picture – Bernard said later that from the boat it looked like Guy Fawkes Night down below – and surfaced.

I should, of course, if I had been a great big bold diver have asked Bernard to run the boat across the estimated course of the big basking shark and gone in with my camera at the ready. It was perhaps particularly galling to hear Colin Doeg many years later tell me how terrified he was when they came across a basking shark off the Devon coast, but how his desire to get the underwater picture of the year forced him into the water.* I suppose that I am just not that dedicated an underwater photographer, and a coward as well.

I was still learning about diving – and about boats as well. I had now replaced the old wreck of a boat that I kept at Bognor Yacht Club with a smart new Fisherman 13, a beautifully made varnished clinker-built boat by Walker of Southend. We were terribly pleased with her as she was obviously a craftsman job and we christened her *Flipper*. With a 4 h.p. Johnson long-shaft on the stern she provided us with a stable diving platform and a boat that was suitable for Bognor's choppy waters.

We now felt a bit millionairish with a boat in both Spain and England, but they did improve not only our holidays but also our week-ends. The papers for the boat in Spain were always a nuisance, but Francisco coped very well with that end. I only hope the time never comes in this country when it is necessary to have to carry papers just to use a boat. The ridiculous thing about all the paperwork in Spain is that the papers merely establish ownership. If they were withheld unless a certified copy of an insurance certificate had to be produced there would be some excuse for them. As it is the Spanish insistence on papers for boats is just pure bureaucracy. Later I was to have cause for saying that with more force. But, despite the papers problem, *Penelope* was a pure delight.

Our holidays in Aiguablava were excellent, not only as regards the diving but because of the hotel too. The waiters were

* His pictures of that basking shark can be seen in *The Underwater Book* (Pelham Books).

a delight. You could be friends with them without having advantage taken of that friendship.

If you think that is a snobby thing to say then I can only reply that you haven't travelled very much. The division between friendship and service is a hair-line. Overstep it from either side – client or waiter – and you have the makings of disaster. But Xiquet Sabater was too intelligent not to employ simpatico men. There was and is no subservience about their service, and most of his staff have been with him for years. I am tempted to write that there are no bad waiters, just bad customers, but that is probably going too far.

Even so I think Xiquet is lucky with his clients – most are intelligent (they have got to be to cope with getting a place in the hotel!) – but then again he holds the whip-hand. A customer who oversteps the line would not get rooms again; a waiter who did the same would be sacked on the spot. And has been. The genius of Xiquet Sabater is that he has been able to bring to middle-class clients the same relationship with a hotel that usually only the very rich can enjoy. The slightest wish is granted if humanly possible – and all this at a price that even I can afford!

While we stayed at the hotel, *Penelope* floated safely at a buoy, watched over by Señor Martin, who is responsible for your boat once you have contracted with him to rent a buoy. I have been grateful for this on many occasions, not the least when the puffy high clouds are pulled apart by winds high up and look like balls of cotton wool pulled out by some woman anxious to get her make-up off. This is a sure sign that a tramontana is on the way.

Then Martin takes control of your boat and if he says it must come in to be hauled up out of the water in his little creek, then in, if you are sensible, it comes. I have always followed Martin's advice. If he says that it would not be a good idea to take the boat outside the bay of Aiguablava then we stay in. If he expresses doubt about the wisdom of running the boat down the coast to San Feliu, then I don't.

Which accounts for the hurried rush Robin and I made one year when we saw the sea was flat calm after we had finished a long lunch. Martin said it was all right, so down the coast we went with no supplies on board except a bottle of

Carlos I brandy. Carlos seems to get better the larger the number which follows the name. (This is the only occasion that I have had to quell a mutiny at sea; 'Check the fuel,' I said – 'Check it yourself,' said Robin hurling an empty brandy bottle into the lake-like sea!)

But the diving at Aiguablava was really good and my camera worked overtime. We found a rock where an octopus would regularly blanch so white at our approach that he looked like a man with a hangover, all white except for the dark circles under his eyes. We examined the underwater slopes of Negra Island just off Cap Bagur because a local fisherman told us that it was crawling with lobsters. Of course it turned out to be the most unlikely lobster country in the world. We found mullet braving the surf for the tit-bits that the sea had washed off. We watched sardines floating in the blue sea in huge schools. Great jellyfish frightened us when we found ourselves finning close to them, but we could still admire their complex structure and gaudy purple trimmings.

We used my aquaplane to skim over the rocks of the bay and search up the sides of Cap Bagur . . . We screamed frantically at water-skiers who seemed to take a delight in coming close and criss-crossing over the silent diver far below.

And came back from all this activity in great visibility to take just as much pleasure – well, almost – in placing lobster pots by hand underwater at Bognor in likely places facing holes that we had seen to shelter shellfish.

Underwater lobster-potting deserves some explanation. Bognor is in some ways unique. It possesses a reef that is almost completely exposed at low tide. Now this may not be extraordinary, but the possession of a reef that is not only left almost high and dry by spring tides, but which is also fairly prolific lobster territory is, to my knowledge, unique in this country. I may well be proved wrong, but as I say if there is another holiday resort in this position I do not know of it.

The lobster pots were much simpler to make than I had first thought.* But putting them down so that no one else could interfere with them was a different matter. The real time to do this was at low tide, so Penny and I heaved and dragged *Flipper* over the mud and clay banks that are part of the

* See *How To Get More Fun From Your Boat* (Pelham Books).

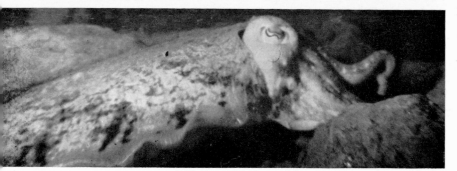

Cuttlefish pictured 60 feet down on the North wall of the Mixon Hole off Selsey Bill, Sussex. There's something really elephantine about the trunk-shaped tentacle, one of many grouped in front of the head and used for capturing prey. This cuttle was about 18 inches long. (*See* Chapter Fifteen)

A big pike in a lake near Coventry. I found that looking up at the surface was the best way to spot these fish. (*See* Chapter Fifteen)

Geoff Bowden, photographed only moments after hand-spearing this 8 lb brill, 40 feet down, on the sand outside the Far Mulberry wreck off Bognor, Sussex. Notice how the flash has bounced back from the white underside of the fish and the appalling visibility. (*See* Chapter Thirteen)

Penny in the wreckage of the Far Mulberry. Notice the shoal of small pouting below and behind her. The darkness on the right is due to the overhang of the wreckage above her. Depth: 35 ft. (*See* Chapter Thirteen)

My favourite of all the pictures of pouting I have taken on the Far Mulberry, off Bognor, Sussex. Notice how every eye is on the photographer. And also that the really big fish have lost their stripes and are now an overall brown, almost black. Depth 40 feet.

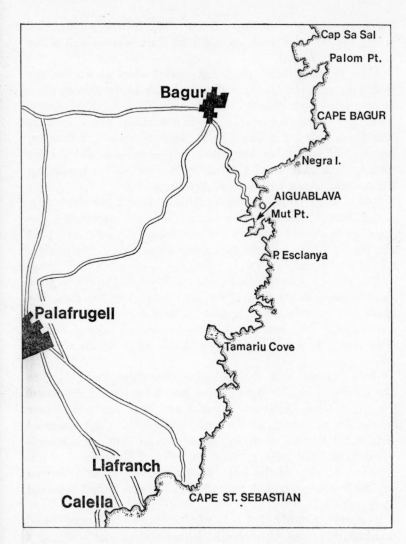

MAP 4. Costa Brava coastline and good diving country. In the north is Cap Sa Sal and the bay of Sa Tuna. Near Palom Point is 'The Place of the Gorgonias'. Aiguablava is a perfect anchorage for anyone who takes a diving boat to the Costa Brava. Near Punta Esclanya is 'Lobster Rock'. And there's a compressor at Calella.

low-water Bognor foreshore. Once afloat it was a matter of poling the boat out with an oar until there was enough water to start the outboard.

Then by using only a mask and snorkel when we reached the reef, I located the lobster holes – or rather likely looking holes in the reef – and placed the pots with their entrance spouts invitingly facing the entrances. The stinking fish I used as bait (fresh bait for crabs; high for lobsters) should, I thought, provide an irresistible temptation. Apparently it did for we took quite a number of lobsters by this method of combining the traditional pot with underwater swimming.

But it wasn't really diving and it all became too much of a fag. I started using floats instead of 'knowing' where the pots were by the use of underwater lines linking the pots. And paid the penalty of letting all and sundry know that I was potting. My pots were smashed up.

We needed a good diving site at Bognor. I spent a great deal of time on research into the shipwrecks in the area. But there just weren't any that sounded as though they would re-pay investigation, and all were too far away – out of reason-able diving range of the Bognor Yacht Club which was our base.

John Messent was now swinging over from spearfishing to the aqualung and he joined in the search for a good site. Local people and local reference libraries and local newspapers (one of the best sources of all) were all terribly helpful, but it seemed a fact that Bognor, as regards shipwrecks in times when records were kept, had just nothing to offer. This seemed extra-ordinary in view of the fact that maps in 1648 found 'Bognor Rocks' important enough to mark, but I gradually had to accept it as true.

However, a study of the Admiralty Chart of the area (2045) marked numerous obstructions. These obstructions were, so I was told, Mulberry units, intended for the D-Day harbour at Arromanches, which had failed to be raised from their parking places when the call came for action. I am now not at all sure that most of the obstructions marked on the chart exist, but John, Robin and a group of Bromley Branch of the British Sub-Aqua Club decided to join in an investigation of the area so that we could pin-point those obstructions worth diving.

A chat with one of the pilots of the rescue helicopters, which are a great comfort to those who sail these waters, confirmed our earlier thoughts that not all the obstructions marked really did exist. The pilot said that he knew of only one dark shape under the sea that could be a sunken Mulberry unit and that was well out to sea from Bognor.

This seemed our best bet and so we loaded *Flipper* up one sunny day with a spare petrol can and the Branch echo-sounder and set off to find this mysterious shape under the sea.

The wreck we were aiming for is marked on the chart as having a warning beacon attached to it, but we knew that if there was such a beacon it was long since gone. Local fishermen knew nothing of it. We searched and searched for the 'wreck' but could not find it. Reg Dunton of Bromley Branch took sextant readings and told us that we must be almost over it, but it seemed a long time before the echo-sounder pen finally went into a powered climb and traced out the outline of something big on the flat seabed round about. Looking down through the water we could see a huge dark shape. But we had no diving equipment with us – a ridiculous oversight – and it wasn't for some weeks that the weather was calm enough for us to use the shore marks we had taken and go out to the 'wreck'.

The day we finally got afloat and out to the Mulberry unit, because that is what it was all right, was one of those days that divers tend to talk about forever after. We took both boats – John's big *Pisces* and my *Flipper* – and we found the Mulberry with no trouble. The shore marks put us on to it – and looking down through the water we could see it.

The divers – John Messent, Reg Dunton, Ray Weddle, David Rose, Malcolm Inch and I – were astounded at what we found. The visibility was well over 30 feet. The sea was blue and the marine life fantastic. Fish swarmed all around us. The wreckage was a marvellous tangle of weed, concrete and iron bars and we thought we were in an aquarium. I used up a whole roll of film in a matter of minutes – one of the pictures won a silver medal in the film competition at the next Brighton Conference of the British Sub-Aqua Club – and it seemed that we couldn't go wrong. We had found our diving site complete with wreckage, fish and good visibility. This was it. This was the Far Mulberry.

Chapter
Thirteen

The Far Mulberry – we always called it that to avoid confusion with the close inshore and smaller unit at Pagham – is a never-ending source of wonder.

No matter how many times we dive there – and over the years our hours underwater on this one site have been considerable – there is always something new to discover.

Each side of the elongated box of concrete which was originally a Phoenix unit of 252 feet long by 60 feet wide and 60 feet high, has something different to show.

On the Admiralty charts the Mulberry is marked as a wreck and shown to have a warning beacon over it. And so it did in 1947 when the chart was brought up to date by Lieutenant J. S. N. Pryor, R.N. and the crew of H.M.M.L. 901 from Portsmouth Command. But the beacon is long since gone and to find it you must know the marks.

We have got rather dab hands at it now and when a certain oddly-shaped tree merges with another behind it and two buildings stand side-by-side, the big outboard is slipped into neutral and there, provided the surface is calm enough, underneath the hull is the great dark shape of the wreck.

I call it a wreck. So do the Navy Hydrographic Department. They decided to do so, I gather, after much discussion. But finally came down on the side of calling it a wreck because it had originally floated, even though strictly speaking it could never have been called a ship.

At low tide on a calm day you can see it clearly. The shape looks brown through the water, mainly because of the long brown fronds of laminaria weed that have engulfed the upper surfaces. On low, low springs I have even seen a frond or two break the surface, but these are attached to an upright iron rod that I suspect carried the missing beacon years ago. Usually, diving at low tide, you will find about 15 feet of

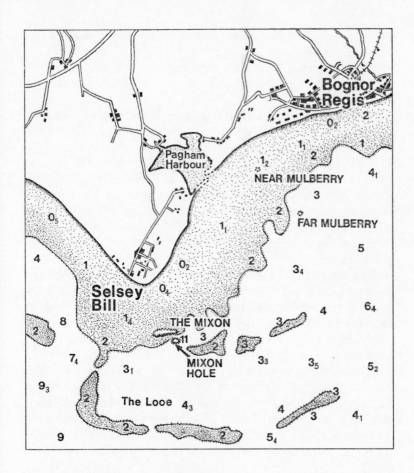

MAP 5. More and more we have concentrated our British diving on the area around Bognor Regis. Both the Near Mulberry and the Far Mulberry are shown. The Mixon Hole is almost exactly due south of the Mixon itself which is marked by a warning beacon. This is an area of very strong tides and great care must be taken when diving.

water over the topmost point. At low tide too there is about 35–40 feet of water down to the seabed at the sunken sides. And as the Phoenix rose 60 feet from flat bottom to the platform on which a Bofors anti-aircraft gun was mounted, she has obviously snuggled some 20 feet into the sand and shingle seabed that now holds her fast.

The diver who is new to the Mulberry will at first find it difficult to visualise the original layout from the tangle that he finds below.

And tangle parts of it certainly are. The storms of a quarter of a century have worked hard to reduce the obstruction to the level of the seabed. In another 50 years they may well succeed.

We wondered when we first explored her about the amount of damage that the unit had suffered. Someone on shore told us that the Navy had put a depth-charge in her, but further enquiries could not confirm this. I think it unlikely particularly as in my research I came across a report of the effect of gales on the Arromanches Harbour for which our Mulberry was intended.

The report in *The Civil Engineer in War*, published by the Institution of Civil Engineers in 1948, says: 'Undoubtedly the severest test which the harbour and its components had to face during the whole period it was in use, was the untimely gale which broke on June 19 and lasted for over three days until June 22, 1944 . . .

'The concrete caissons did not fare so well. The gale coincided with spring tides and at high-water the heavy seas sweeping along the length of the units in the detached mole filled the more deeply placed ones with water whose only means of subsequent escape was through the open seacocks and a number of ports provided for the purpose just above the lower-deck level.

'The rate of escape was quite inadequate to keep pace with the fall in the outside water-level as trough succeeded crest, so that the units were subjected to an internal hydrostatic pressure, nearly rhythmic in its application and of an intensity which their walls were not calculated to withstand. As a result of that treatment, several of the units burst and disintegrated.'

When I read that I knew what had happened to our Mulberry all alone out there in the gales of winter after winter.

What is she like now? Well let's dive down and see. First of all one of us slings in a light grapnel with six foot of chain before the rope. Then while we get kitted up we let the slack take up.

At one time we got careless about our diving procedure and in would go both the grapnel and a heavier anchor. The first divers down would check each one to see that it was firmly into the wreckage and then the other divers in the boat would go in together, leaving the boat, as we thought, so firmly moored that nothing but a typhoon would break it free.

But carelessness costs lives – where boats and diving are concerned and we could have lost ours or had a very long swim back to shore but for a stroke of luck.

On the day that it happened there was a strong south-west wind blowing and though the boat was riding easily to the waves every now and then she would snub hard on the anchor ropes. At the last minute when we were all kitting up to go in Malcolm Todd, who had already dived earlier on the Mixon Hole, decided to stay in the boat as he had very little air left.

I dived, John Messent dived and so did Geoff Bowden. The anchors were checked and we set off round the Mulberry. On our return to the anchor rope at the end of the dive we were surprised to find only the grapnel down and this was tied to the frayed ends of the main anchor warp. But it wasn't until we got back into the boat that the full story of our luck came out.

Malcolm Todd had been sitting in the boat tidying up the mess of equipment ready for the run back to Bognor. As he worked he noted that the wind had fallen – or so he thought – and that the sea was definitely calmer. After sorting out the boat to his satisfaction he glanced towards the shore and to his surprise noted that the boat was well off the marks. He went forward to check the anchor and pulled in a rope that had been cut clean through. He checked the grapnel and found that it was bumping along the bottom.

The boat had drifted with the wind for at least a mile, but starting the engine and motoring back on to the marks was a simple matter. He then tied the grapnel on to the main anchor rope, hooked it into the Mulberry and waited for us to finish our dive.

All very simple – except for two things. One, it was sheer chance that he decided to stay in the boat. And two, it was just his second trip to the Mulberry and John Messent had only told him the marks that morning during idle conversation.

If either of those two things had not happened, even with our diving life-jackets we should have been hours in the water before making the shore or being picked up. Surfacing and not finding a boat, but miles of empty sea all round, has always been one of my diving nightmares. That time it nearly came true. Now someone always stays in the boat, for the sharp edges of the Mulberry can cut through thicker ropes than ours. We've found four fishing boat anchors there to date.

But back to finding out what the Mulberry looks like underwater. The grapnel is tightly in now and the boat is anchored just off the northern or shoreward end of the wreckage. Visibility, of course, varies and can be 50 feet. Well out to sea as we are it rarely goes below 10 feet. So we can see what we're about.

Looking down on a Phoenix unit when it was brand-new was like looking down on the top of a gigantic egg-box. It was divided into a mass of small compartments to give the concrete structure strength.

This strengthening was in addition to the hundreds of iron reinforcing rods that were laced throughout. The compartments interconnected with water-channels to aid in settling the unit on an even keel when flooded-down in position.

Down the anchor rope to check the grapnel. Not such a good shot this one. It ought to be farther to the west and now we'll have to fin down among the weed to make sure that it is into something substantial and not just hooked by one fluke around a rusting rod that will give way with just a little pressure.

We're over the middle of the Mulberry and in the gaps in the carpet of green weed, those dark grey holes are the compartments. The floor of each is a mass of rusting rods and corroded debris. We drift down into one and long green pollack shift to one side, keeping big gold-rimmed eyes on us to make sure we don't come too close. Pollack, more than most fish, seem sensitive to sudden noise and usually move away fast at the rush of bubbles from the demand valves as you exhale. The tide is running very gently for the pollack to be around here; when it gets stronger they'll move to the shelter of the opposite side of the wreck.

This northern end of the unit is best preserved, but even so the western compartments have broken down there leaving more of a slope down to the seabed than a sheer wall. As we start down towards the sand on the western side you can already see the black outlines of hundreds of fish below. These are bib, or pouting.

As we get closer they hardly bother to move away and the youngsters are all light vertical stripes over the pale brown of the body colour. The bigger ones – and they're not worried either – are a deeper brown all over. The light stripes of the immature fish are gone and the brown is so dark on some of the biggest ones of nearly two feet long that you could fairly call it black.

Part of the upper wall of the Mulberry lies separated from the main structure here where the waves have ripped it free. Only a narrow channel, where you'll sometimes spot a lobster or two or three fat red mullet scuffling in the sand for food, separates it from the main mass. This is a favourite spot for the pouting. Even when the tide runs hard from the west they congregate in a packed mass of several hundred fish behind the shelter of this broken-off piece.

They're not frightened of you. Of course, they keep an eye on you and each photograph you take of them will show that every eye is looking at you, but you can literally touch them. They don't like it and jump forward a foot, but if the tide is strong that's all they do and then let themselves drift back into position with the rest.

We've taken great care not to frighten these fish. They are part of the charm of the Mulberry and though any brute could run the big ones through with a short handspear, we've made sure that the temptation is resisted.

If the tidal movement runs through the channel you won't find many pouting there. They'll all have moved along a bit towards the north where a great overhang provides better shelter. The reason for this overhang is a bit hard to work out. It looks like a great dark cave and I suspect that tidal scour has broken away the side of the Mulberry and the over-hang is really the inside of the outer compartments. Still it looks an eerie place and is usually the home of giant wrasse and really big old pouting.

Further on still heading north we turn the corner of the bow (or is it the stern?). Both ends of the Mulberry units were very similar. I secretly suspect that what we call the bow is really the stern, for if she sank when just starting her tow to the D-Day beaches surely her bow would be heading out to sea, not pointing square at the shore as it does now?

At any rate the 'bow' is a gloomy place. Here a few real rocks litter the seabed, but all the rest is shingle right up to the angle where it meets the concrete. Here, too, you would never suspect that the structure is made of concrete for thousands of white and orange deadmen's fingers completely cover its surface. The white polyps of the anemones which are open – and at any time there are hundreds that are – give, at first sight, a ghostly glow to the Noah's Ark type of bow that shelves out above you.

Under its angle on the shingle there are usually one or two starfish, hunched up over some luckless mussel that has lost its hold above.

At the end of the bow, there is a sharp, clear-cut corner and the run down the eastern side begins. The unit on this side is for the first 50 feet better preserved than anywhere else. The wall towers up sheer almost to the top. Vent pipes open down close to the seabed and offer dark hiding places.

You would think that these are the ideal places for lobster or some monstrous conger, but though I look in each time I fin past there is never anything inside. Neither does the outer wall provide much other cover for fish or shellfish. The wall itself is covered, like everything else that remains of the Mulberry, with growth, but here it has not gained so much of a foothold. The weeds and sponge-encrustation are short and not until you rise up to meet the green and brown canopy of laminaria that hangs down from the top do you find the sort of places where sea creatures like to hide.

The seabed at the foot of the eastern wall changes character as we move along it. Increasingly weed sprouts from the seabed. When the sun is penetrating well through the water it looks at times like fields of corn with the golden tips of the pod-weed glowing in the light.

But after 50 or 60 feet the wall gives way to the sea. The impression of a prison wall turns into a tumble and a tangle of weeds and collapsed compartments with rods poking this way and that from each hummock of debris.

In fact the further South you go, the more the unit loses its identity. Here and there you find a recognisable piece of wall collapsed, but still standing proud of the seabed.

Or in another few yards a piece flat on its side, but the true shape of the unit is difficult to follow. The sand must cover huge sections for the weed sprouts from the seabed in great profusion and it cannot do that unless its holdfasts have found something solid beneath the sand.

Back down the western side then and into a mass of slabs of wreckage. It is here that a blue-faced conger pokes out its head from one particular hole, though there must be many more deep in the dark recesses that no diver could ever penetrate. Every now and then one of us sees the head of a real monster, but he never seems to be in the same place and so perhaps we are not reporting the same fish. The cold-eyed stare and Great Dane head of a big conger doesn't make for cool reporting. Very occasionally you come across one out for a stroll among the weed forests at the southern end, but as this is usually on late dives in fading light all the real conger activity probably begins at night.

That then is what the Mulberry looks like on just a quick trip round. In itself the wreck is not sensational. No sunken treasure, no souvenir portholes, no ghostly steering wheel, no silent engines. But it is the life that surrounds it that provides the real thrill.

Since our first dive on the Mulberry over five years ago – when the concrete jungle made us think that the unit had capsized and was lying on its side – every visit has brought us something new.

I remember a great blue lobster moving out into the open and walking calmly from one side of a compartment to the other. I still see one compartment that has a huge heap of empty mussel shells in one corner. What makes them settle there? What trick of current flutters them to that particular spot? Or is there some giant mussel-eater hidden in the weed round about? I confess that I proceed with caution each time I find myself exploring the area near that rubbish tip.

My log-book entries seem to consist mainly of 'Far Mulberry', the date, and masses of notes on what we saw there. I remember the 10-pound lobster, not blue but solid grey with growths all over him, that Reg Dunton took by hand from the section that has fallen clear on the western side. Its claws were bigger than my hands and as the magnification of the size of shellfish underwater is well known to divers (officially one-third, but shellfish always seem bigger!), I envied Reg his courage in picking it up.

I still have the photographs of bright red deadmen's fingers that live in one compartment – and which really shouldn't be there because they usually only survive in the sheltered waters of a Norwegian fiord.

Photographs too of the bass who couldn't care less. From his size he must have been well into double figures, but he didn't behave like other British bass. In the open if you come on a bass, he is unlikely to stay around for long. Often you can see a dark shape almost at the limit of visibility for some time, but you'll rarely get close to the same fish again.

This bass was the exception. He came swimming along the eastern side of the Mulberry, along the sheer wall, and almost bumped into Penny who was a little ahead of me. In fact I was still out of sight of her behind the corner of the overhang. When she came finning back to me indicating with wide open arms that there was a huge fish just around the corner, I finned forward without much hope of seeing it. Big fish don't usually hang around for second looks at divers. But there he was! And he appeared as interested in us as we were in him. I held my breath for as long as I could as I got the camera up to my eye, but then just had to breathe out.

Now normally that would have been enough to send the fish hurtling out of sight. But not this one. He seemed even more curious and came so close that I could count the scales above the lateral line on his side.

I let off a flash-bulb almost in his face. He flicked around in a circle and as I fumbled frantically for another bulb, passed between Penny and I and we were side by side in the water! I got the flash-bulb in and then he decided to swim between the wall of the Mulberry and the camera and I had time for a real close-up. After that he had had enough, but even then his flight was no panic just a leisurely finning with that thick powerful tail forcing his blunt-looking head with its big mouth against the slight southerly current.

It was only after he had gone that I remembered the warnings of other underwater photographers that photographing a bass with flash was like trying to outline a half-crown against a white sheet. In fact it is true that those pictures did show a glow surrounding the fish where the flash had bounced back from silver scales which act as hundreds of tiny mirrors.

Bass, of course, are hunters and are often to be found around the Mulberry. This is not in the least surprising as the food supplies around it are prodigious. And though the bass generally like searching the weedy surfaces for tiny soft crabs and similar tasty morsels the huge schools of pouting – ranging from a few inches in size up to 'monsters' of about two feet – must come in for some weeding when hungry bass swoop in.

The pouting have provided me with many engrossing hours. They are one of the commonest of British fish in the south-east and one rarely dives in that area without seeing them. On the Mulberry they crowd together in schools of over 200 fish and there seems to be no stand-offishness about them. They will happily merge with pollack schools if the pollack want it. One gets the distinct impression that the pollack, green and streamlined, consider themselves a cut above the pouting or at least that they swim together when the pollack want it and not as a general rule.

The pollack seems too a more sensitive fish than the pouting. A quickly exhaled breath with its resultant rush of bubbles and noise from the demand valve will often send a pollack flying away.

The pouting on the other hand is not so liable to take fright and a cloud of bubbles may well bring the school even closer to investigate. Or will only make the fish withdraw a few feet.

If you let a flash-bulb off close to a pollack underwater he may well go into a raring tizzy of flight. The pouting will take a flash-bulb right in the face without apparently even noticing the blaze of light. The pouting is curious about you; the pollack suspicious and though both fish will let the diver close the pollack will be the first to insist that you keep your distance by moving away himself.

The reference books on fish have often got the coloration of the pouting wrong – 'a copper colouring with dark cross-bands' says one. The pouting is in fact a dark fish with light cross-bands. And this only applies to the young fish. When they are a few inches long they all bear the bands and some quite large fish up to about a foot in length will have this banding. But the bigger older fish will always be a uniform dark copper colour and in some cases this coloration is so dark that the fish is almost black. Most books too suggest that a foot-long fish is a big one. This is untrue. Big pouting are nearly two feet long.

And this is where the bigger fish differ in their behaviour from the younger ones. The big pouting are more restrained than the youngsters – and this seems quite natural. Natural too is their habit of grouping together according to size with the big ones leading a school and the little ones bringing up the rear.

In fact when the tide is running hard and the south-west side of the Mulberry is the sheltered side the big pouting will shelter together and let the youngsters go elsewhere. Four or five whoppers then line up and hang almost immobile in the shelter of some broken piece of wreckage. It takes a lot in this situation to make them move. Cameras shoved almost into their noses have little effect. Flash-bulbs exploding none at all. I have touched them and found that they jump nervously forward a foot or two, but return to their position in line like battle-ships while the smaller cruisers and destroyers criss-cross and turn around their formation.

Other old pouting seem to like the twisting tunnels and holes inside the Mulberry. They glide about there without much concern for the underwater intruder who peers in at them. They share these retreats with big cuckoo wrasse, who react much more violently to close-up observation and speed away with a flurry of disturbed water.

I was peering into one of these holes on one dive when I realised that I was looking right through a tangle of girders and out into a glade of drooping weed. Something kept flashing at the limit of visibility and for a moment or two I thought I was looking through at John Messent or Malcolm Todd. The flashing I thought was caused by one of the white and black quarters on the neck of a British aqualung bottle which denotes that it contains compressed air.

But the white flashing was too jerky and I pushed as far forward as I could without getting hooked up on wreckage to see what it was. The flashing came towards me then and I saw that it was a fish.

I was watching the death of a big pouting. It seemed un-damaged except that it was swimming in circles on its side. The white flashing was the white underbelly of the fish jerking through the water. And it was jerking and twitching as though in spasm. The circles got smaller and smaller and finally the fish flopped on its side and lay twitching among the short weed that carpeted the glade. It made what could only be described as two arching efforts to get back on to its fins and then lay still. I couldn't get right in to examine it closely, but it looked completely unwounded, bitten or even scratched.

Before this I had noted several of the pouting – especially the bigger ones – had some white growth around the mouth. It doesn't seem to affect them, though in one advanced case I saw the fish swim with its mouth open all the time and, I suspect, could not close it. It looks like some sort of fungus and is, more than likely, the result of pollution. Though whether this sort of disease could be directly attributed to the way we are pouring sewage and debris of all kinds into the sea, only a scientific examination of the fish can tell.

I suppose with all the fish there are in those schools around the Mulberry it is surprising that I have only noticed one really oddly-marked pouting. This one was completely dark brown like all the big ones except for a broad white stripe running from the back of its head near start of the main dorsal fin diagonally backwards behind the gill cover right down to the fish's belly. The fish appeared active and looked sleek and I don't know the reason for the mark. I thought at first it might be some mating colouration, but then I would have been bound to see the same thing on other fish. Perhaps one of his light bands slipped in his youth and stuck like it! At any rate I took a photograph of it for record purposes.

Speaking of taking photographs of pouting (or bib as they are often called), each time I dive on the Mulberry I swear I won't take another picture of a pouting, but somehow sooner or later I find the huge schools impossible to resist and each reel of 35 m.m. High Speed Ektachrome that goes through my Nikonos camera on the Mulberry contains at least one shot of them.

The camera is always with me when I dive on the Mulberry because you can never be sure what you are going to find there. Early in the season you can often spot a cod low down among the pouting schools. If you stir up some of the seabed with your flippers this is the pouting's idea of a real good turn and they swoop in and pick up the goodies that my eye cannot see, but which theirs obviously can.

The pouting take kindly to feeding. Their favourite seems to be a well-known brand of cat food. But I have news for the expert sea-angler who confidently wrote that all sea fish like boiled rice. The pouting don't. In fact they swim through a cascade of it without showing the slightest interest. Penny took down a whole plastic bag full in the hope of having the fish eating literally out of her hand, but it was a miserable failure. But we haven't finished our experiments yet. Perhaps next year we'll find the magic all-purpose fish food.

Most divers have a peculiar set of rules about the undersea world. It is not the done thing to spearfish using an aqualung – even though there is no law against it in Britain. But there is, it seems, no objection to using a short handspear or even a diving knife to take a 'flattie' when wearing a lung. Lobsters and crabs too are fair game – provided they are taken by hand or with the assistance of a hooked rod. Spearing them is just not on.

It is amazing how quickly the diver accepts these unwritten laws. On most dives when not encumbered by underwater camera, lightmeter, flash-bulbs and various close-up lenses, I carry a 'prodder'. Now the fact that the 'prodder' is quite conveniently turned into a handspear doesn't make any difference to the fact that I would willingly spear a flat fish with the 'prodder', but would certainly not do the same thing with a speargun – nor would I carry one with a lung. It seems completely illogical, but the fact remains that to carry a speargun with aqualung equipment is just not on.

The truth of this came home to me when we made a late dive in October one year on the Far Mulberry. There was a strong south-west wind. Over the Mulberry this had built up a ten-foot swell.

We had put the grapnel well into the wreckage, but the boat was snubbing so hard against the anchor rope after each wave had passed that we all knew someone must stay in the boat. In fact conditions were so bad that I had grave doubts about the advisability of diving at all. John Messent volunteered to stay in the boat while Geoff Bowden and I dived – and that fact alone convinced me that John thought there was a good chance of the boat breaking free.

Well, the sooner we are in, I thought, the sooner we can call it a day. Geoff Bowden and I rolled in one after another linked up ten feet down and then moved across the Mulberry towards the south-east, down a crack in the side to the sand below. Once under and down a bit the calm bore no relation to the turmoil of sea on the surface. In fact within a few moments you forgot the roughness up above. The tide was running at about two to three knots but on this side we were in comparatively sheltered water. Visibility was poor – almost the poorest I have seen on the Mulberry – about six feet. I despaired of being able to photograph anything, but extreme close-ups with flash.

I had reckoned, however, without Geoff Bowden's sharp eyes. He stopped dead as we swam side by side along the wall and examined the sand beneath him closely.

I had just time – and only just – to note two eyes and a big oval shape in the sand before his handspear plunged downward – and a 12 pound turbot was fluttering frantically away on the end of the barb. I use the word 'fluttering'. Jerking would be a more apt description and I managed to bang off one or two flash-bulbs before Geoff had the turbot inside a sack that he pulled out from under the bottom edge of his wet suit top. It was a highly complicated manoeuvre which involved unscrewing the head of the handspear to release the fish. When he had got it in the sack and was firmly clasping the edges of the sack shut, the whole sack started to swim away and was only restrained by his grasp round the un-occupied end.

But more was to come. We had only gone a yard more when the same performance took place except that this time the victim was an eight pound brill that I didn't even notice on the sand. The sack now was positively mobile and jerked away from Geoff in violent attempts to escape.

Whether it was the time of the year – which I suspect – or the poor visibility – which I suspect too – there was no doubt that the Mulberry that day was seething with fish.

Huge schools of large pollack and pouting circled around us. The fish were the largest I had seen there and I wondered if at the end of the year the fish gathered in tight to the Mulberry in some form of defensive ring. Certainly four or five big bass were swimming in amongst the fish and though they showed no aggressive tendencies at that moment there was no doubt what would happen if hunger moved them.

Then it was my turn to see flatfish. From right underneath my nose a great big plaice exploded from the sand and, before I could swing the camera up, proceeded to behave the way I had seen no plaice behave before. Usually a plaice when disturbed moves on some distance and then settles down to the seabed to sink into the sand and hope that it will escape notice. This one was different. It swam towards the wall of the Mulberry, went into a vertical climb, zoomed right up to the top and then, with Kendall and camera in hot pursuit, dipped down into section after section of the Mulberry's egg-boxes before disappearing into the gloom on the other side. Here I lost sight of the fish as I came into the full force of the tide. In the grey-green mist I lost him and swung back – or rather was swept back over the Mulberry – in time to drop back into shelter.

The swim after the plaice I knew had sopped up air. I had felt myself drawing in great gulps of it. I looked at Geoff who was still struggling with his sackful of fish. I pointed up and shrugged my shoulders in a question. He nodded and we went up. We broke surface quite close to the boat and though from that level the waves looked quite alarming it was impossible to interpret the height of the swell until you actually grasped hold of the boat. As each wave came you rose up and then the wave fell away leaving your legs almost free of the water.

We scrambled in – and as we did so the anchor rope parted like a snapping bowstring. John started the engine and headed us into the sea. It was time to go home. The last dive of that season had been quite an event.

Chapter
Fourteen

It would be difficult to imagine finding a spot as prolific with sea life as our Bognor Mulberry wreck and one that was so handy to a boating base. But after several years of going to Aiguablava on holiday we managed it.

This diving spot was not a wreck just a rock. But what a rock! From the north side seabed at 50 feet it soars upwards rather as the Llosa near San Feliu did, but breaks the surface and shows three feet of weed-encrusted rock for all to see. When the winds blow spray breaks without effort over it, but you are still aware that it is there by the white foam the waves leave behind.

All I am going to say here is that it is near Punta Esclanya and even if you use a photographic blow-up, as I do, of the small-scale admiralty chart of the area you will not see it marked. It is inside the towering cliffs of one of the little bays between Tamariu and Aiguablava, but that will be of little help to anyone searching for our favourite Spanish diving spot as there are a profusion of little bays between the two points.

I am not being mean in refusing to share the exact location, but this rock seems to be the favourite haunt of baby spiny lobsters and someone's stomach might overcome his feelings for my photography! There may well be other rocks just as interesting as this one in the area for it is good diving country. And perhaps the pleasure we have found in diving there comes from going back again and again to the same spot.

This really underlines the mistake that many divers and snorkellers make. They are always looking for new places and never seem to devote any real amount of time to one good spot. Perhaps we were lucky on our first dive on 'Lobster Rock' to find the yellow-and-red barred antennae of spiny lobsters poking out at us in profusion from holes only 40 feet down.

This really riveted our attention to the rock. And to be honest, my first thought was that here was a meal to rival those splendid *á la carte* dishes that the chef at the Aigua Blava Hotel sends out into the dining-room to tempt the *pension* customers to desert their budgets.

I was wary, however, about their size. I had no wish to break the law in Spain about undersize lobsters – a similar law to the one we have been careful to observe in all our diving in Britain. And from experience I know how big shellfish tend to look underwater and how disappointing their real size is when they are out of the water and in a specimen net in the diving boat.

So that first year we found the lobsters, Penny and I carefully selected the largest of them all – his 'feelers' were fully two feet long – and by grasping the antennae very close to the head pulled the spiny creature from his hole.

The use the lobster makes of the antennae is interesting. I found that if you put your gloved hand near the lobster the antennae would wave down and feel around your fingers. This exploration by touch – some experts believe a sense of smell is there in the antennae too – produced no visible alarm in the lobster.

The next step was to grab the antennae close to the head to prevent the brittle twig-like material from snapping. This grab provokes instant reaction. The lobster will struggle desperately to get back into the hole by the use of its powerful tail snapping up under its body and by a scrabbling action of the legs on which it stands. A sentimentalist would let go at this stage, but if you hold on the pressure each way becomes equal and the affair seems to reach a stalemate.

Continued pressure by the diver seems to tire the lobster and suddenly with a rush the creature is out in open water. Then the powerful tail comes into full play and the lobster jerks and jerks at the end of your grasp.

This is the moment of risk for the would-be captor. The violent jerking, and it is violent, can result in the antennae breaking and the lobster rushing backwards free. If this happens it will not go far and if no hole is immediately handy will flatten itself against the nearest rock and apparently invite a fresh onslaught.

The rusty red of the lobster's carapace – that part of its

shell from the two spikes at the front over the eyes to the point where the flexible tail fits in – is then displayed to full advantage and the blue colouration around the edge of the fan of the tail is particularly beautiful.

In the one that Penny and I selected one of the antennae broke a long way up and the creature rested calmly in my grasp across its back – I was glad of the gloves because the carapace is thornier than a rose bush – while Penny measured its carapace and tail against a steel ruler that I carry in my diving bag for just such a purpose. Despite its apparent size the lobster was only eight inches from eyes to tail. We let it go close to its hole – almost backed it in – and concentrated on counting the others in the immediate vicinity. There were eight in the space of one overhang and more here and there in cracks in the sheer rock.

But the joy of Lobster Rock was not just in its lobsters. In all my Mediterranean diving from Sicily to Spain and back again I have never seen such a variety of marine life as that rock displayed.

Great brown-blotched white sea-slugs (*Peltodoris atromaculata*) fed on purple sponges, leaving circular white scars where they had eaten their way right through. Red sea squirts (*Halocynthia papillosa*) were so common they were a positive plague. Red growth was everywhere, most of it the veined sponge called *Hymeniacidon sanguinea*, and great yellow boughs of *Axinella polypoides* would jut out from cracks in crags near the base of the rock at 50 feet. Great golden rains of anemones (*Parazoanthus axinellae*) covered the undersides of overhangs and among them were the delicate shapes of Neptune's baskets and pen worms in full plumage and fan worms and . . . well I could go on for ever.

There was enough growth on that rock to keep all the world's marine biologists happy for at least a year. I have used the Latin names of many of them, not to illustrate how clever I am – any fool can look them up in a book – but to leave no doubt about the species I am writing about. There really are no common names for most of these commonly seen things, though perhaps that is just as well. The Latin names were given for just this purpose – so that there can be no doubt that we are all describing the same thing.

So far I have, of course, not described the fish population of that rock. This varies with the season, but generally the rock was home to hundreds of blennies, which slithered forward with curiosity at the diver's close approach. There were all kinds of wrasse there too and it was clear that some kind of territory was marked out for each, but it would take more research than my holiday allowed time for even a start to be made on sorting that out.

The adults of the chromis family – the ones years ago I first heard called 'the flies of the sea' – had in late July the firmest views about territory on Lobster Rock. The crack or cleft that each had chosen for its own was, if invaded, the sign for an onslaught that bears little comparison to the size of the fish. The 'big' ones are a deeper purple than the youngsters and dark black dot-like stripes cover the body. Their attack on some hapless wrasse who strayed into forbidden territory was made up of a purple streak and a butting and a thumping that drove the intruder far away. I was interested to see if these little fish would take on a black wet-suited diver when I peered close into some cleft in which the chromis, flattened against some rock, busily fanned away to keep in position. But they ignored me. I have no doubt that some scientist will put me right when I say that I couldn't see the reason for this territorial stake-out. I got within inches in my search for eggs – for the defence of those could account for such aggression – but could see none. The chromis did not attack even such close intrusion, but stayed in position.

Lobster Rock was, however, the real domain of the scorpion fish. There are two common kinds in the Mediterranean – *Scorpaena porcus*, which is reddish brown and grows up to about 25 c.m. in length, and *Scorpaena scrofa*, which is more or less the same colour, but is bigger (up to 40 c.m.) and which lives up to its name by looking absolutely scrofulous.

The rock held both. And both female and male of both species. The female always looks smaller and darker than the male.

In fact, you had to be jolly careful where you put your hands when photographing close to the rock face. Many times I have just been about to grip a projecting outcrop when I have noticed that close to it was the highly-camouflaged simulated growth-covered body of one or the other species. No fish that I know signals its poisonous nature in so clear a way as the scorpion fish – even at first sight it looks dangerous.

But scorpion fishes do make a highly photogenic subject. All I would suggest to would-be photographers of this fish is that before settling down before the immobile fish – they will not move until closely threatened – they should check the surrounding scenery which parts of their body are likely to touch. The female of the species can often be found within a few feet of the male. The sting from the dorsal spines of male or female can be a case for hospital treatment.

The rock is something extraordinary in that particular area. I have searched the walls of the bay on both sides of the rock and found them barren in comparison. Perhaps some current full of nutrient supplies that rock. Perhaps some upwelling of food from deeper down – the water just outside the bay is over 30 metres deep and just a little further goes from 52 to 109 metres – feeds all the life on Lobster Rock. Or perhaps like our Mulberry two miles off the Sussex coast the rock is a focal point in a comparatively barren area. I don't know. But I do know that diving there is a delight.

We have, as I wrote earlier, gone back there year after year and little is changed. But we have been able to watch some things expand. I am thinking particularly of the spiny lobsters. After measuring the biggest one I went to look for him again the next year. He wasn't there. I felt like a murderer. Had breaking his antenna made him easy prey for some predator? Had the shock been so much that he had decided to move on? How had the colony of baby lobsters established itself there anyway? Didn't spiny lobsters behave the same way as their Cornish cousins and go deep at some time in their life?

I didn't know the answers to any of those questions and it seems to me, after some research, that few scientists would know the answers either. In Cornwall we had not usually found the crawfish in depths of under 60 feet and divers had reported seeing long lines of them in the spring walking in from the deeps.

Yet here I was with a colony of babies at 40–50 feet and, as far as I could see, only one missing. The one that I had hauled out his hole the year before.

I gave up looking for him – all the others had both their antennae intact and seemed to about the same in number as the year before – and started to circle Lobster Rock in an anti-clockwise direction. I knew what I would see. The rock was lop-sided as regards depth. On the side opposite the north wall of the bay the lobsters lived. On the pointed end nearest the shore the depth on the north remained at about 45 feet and then on the southern side plunged down to 80 feet. Swimming along the comparatively-barren southern side you found the depth increasing slowly as you came towards the seaward point, but when you rounded that and shelved upwards back to the northern side, the rock became progressively more interesting.

I made a circuit and then in order to get back to the anchor rope and *Penelope*, which hardly moved in the calm of the bay, passed the lobster ground and headed once more towards the shore.

It was on this second run over the ground with the rock face hard on my left that I spotted him. There was no doubt that it was my missing lobster. One antennae was broken off about half-way up and I recognised him immediately. In distance he was about 60 feet from our first meeting and though I keep calling him 'he', he might well have been a 'she'. In my delight at finding him again I forgot, as I had the first time, to examine his underside and make sexing positive.

I signalled to Penny and she understood at once, finning up to the boat and returning with the metal ruler. Gently, ever so gently I pulled him from his hole. Nine inches! In one year he had grown only one inch. So much for those who believe that a spiny lobster sheds at least twice a year and doubles his size in a year when young.

It was then that my lobster chirped. There is no other way to describe it and underwater it sounded just like a distress call. If there had been any justice in the undersea world a giant lobster would have answered that pitiful call and snatched the baby back to freedom.

I held the lobster close to my face mask and the chirping continued. It was not a high-pitched sound, but a sort of beep of low alarm. Close to there was no doubt of the linkage that made the noise. The undamaged antennae – my hand was right around the body – was moving up and down like a clockwork toy soldier's arm and on each up stroke the bleep came loud and clear. I have read that the scientists say that this noise is caused by the rubbing of the antennae on the carapace and I won't argue with this diagnosis. But even close to I couldn't see the point of contact.

I took the baby back to a suitable hole in the original rock face that he had called home. Next year I will check on him again.

However the rock was not only fascinating because of the colony of lobsters. One particularly fine day – the sea was so calm that the wake of the *Penelope* was the only disturbance on the cliffs that we passed – we came back again to Lobster Rock. On the way ripples on the water here and there were quite clearly caused by fish jumping and at one point Kevin and Joanna pointed out a 'flight' of tiny fish that jumped and skittered over the surface before falling back with quite audible plops into the flat oily surface.

It was already hot and a thin wraith of mist began to crown the head of Cap Bagur. Both Penny and I slipped on wet suit tops before we dived – slipped is the right word for every movement brought on a fine sweat – for we knew that though the surface water would be warm in its stillness, further down the sea temperature was bound to be shivery.

I was using a 65 cu. ft. negatively buoyant bottle, one of two that I had borrowed before we set out from England. These extra bottles gave us one more dive before we were forced to go into either Palamos or Calella to refill them all.

The thing about using negatively buoyant bottles one day and positively buoyant bottles the next is that you should alter your weight belt to suit each one. This in practice proved an awful fiddle and so I was prepared to keep the weightbelt the same and blow a little air into my lifejacket to compensate when using the negatively buoyant one. Even so it was difficult to get the amount of air in the life-jacket just right – I was not using the Fenzy life-jacket which is so easy to adjust for weight and depth – and rather than over-inflate I tended to be still overweight.

This meant I had a tendency to sink unless I kept finning

steadily. Doing this with a non-compressed air life-jacket is against all the rules and is a silly practice – if you needed suddenly to fully inflate the jacket by means of the gas cylinder you could easily over-inflate and burst the buoyancy bag. Still I did it even though I knew it was wrong.

But this sinking feeling did mean that it was better to avoid long periods over deep water as finning all the time is very tiring. So I worked round the south side of Lobster Rock where there were several shelves which, provided you made sure you didn't settle on the spines of a sea-urchin, you could use as a resting place. Penny who was using a positively buoyant cylinder glided along to my right over deep water with her weights so well adjusted that she could regulate her height in the water by just a flick of her fins.

It was while we were working along the south side that I saw the 'whitebait' – not that you could have missed seeing them they were there in such massive quantities. I call them whitebait, but all I can be sure of is that they were the fry of some fish – tiny transparent creatures with their orange-red intestines showing clearly through the skin.

The water was thick with them, but they were not just drifting. They shot this way and that in unison as though someone was pulling one of those beaded curtains to and fro in great sweeps.

It was an amazing sight and I lay on a rock shelf at the seaward end of the rock just watching what was going on. It was like having a grandstand seat at some primitive tribal ceremony. For those little fish were not sweeping backwards and forwards for fun – they were being hunted. And hunted without mercy. Looking into the dark blue deep down, the fishy curtain was even more agitated and big flashes of silver told what was going on down there.

I looked to my right and Penny was spread-eagled on the surface of another flat shelf looking down just as I was. I knew from the stillness of her position that she was as transfixed by the sight as I was. It was while looking to my right that I saw the bass begin his first run into the shoal. He circled for a moment, his sides looking greeny-grey in the light near the surface and then he plunged into the wall of fish. Where he hit the tiny fish they jerked a bit and he must have swallowed dozens, but it made not the slightest impression on the thousands there.

In some way the little fish seemed almost to ignore the bass's attacks – as though he was a minor problem. It was clear that something else was causing the panic. And it wasn't the shoal of sardines that suddenly plunged down from above for a feed like a flight of silver darts. They too seemed insignificant.

There was no doubt in my mind that what we were watching was some sort of feeding frenzy. The water almost boiled and at times the curtain of fish was drawn right across us so that Penny disappeared from my view and the water all around me was just a mass of pinky blobs and black eyes and transparent bodies.

When this happened and the royal blue of the deep was almost obliterated by fish and they covered the sides of the rock itself, the sars would join in chasing the tiny fry. It looked to me as though the sars were hardly interested in eating the fry, but merely chased them out of sheer sadistic pleasure.

These attacks by the sars split the fry closest to them into small groups for a few moments before the main body would envelop these isolated pockets. The bass came in again and cruised past close enough for me to photograph – at other times he was hidden by fish – and through the frame-finder I could see the bass eating as he went along.

Now the fry started to go mad and the curtain of them swished more and more violently. Something big was obviously coming and I looked down again expecting to see something huge come up from the depth where the silver flashes were still lighting up the blue-black of the sea.

But the creatures that caused the fry to panic most came not from down below, but from the extreme left of my vision. At first they were dim silver shapes and then as the tiny fish parted in front of them, their outline became quite clear. Two big dentex, deep silver fish, looking at least three feet long. Closer still they came and then they were right in front of me. I managed to get the camera up and let off a flash bulb, but they had no fear of me or the flash and they powered their way through the fry munching as they went along. They seemed completely unconcerned like two undertakers out for a stroll and having a snack as they glided along. Then they were gone and the fry closed in after them.

I waited for them to come back, but they didn't, and the other fish went on killing and the sea swayed and boiled with tiny creatures desperately trying to survive. The bass killed and killed and the silver flashed all around from the white surface water down to the navy blue of the deep.

I lay there until my air ran out and almost had to pull Penny away from her perch as I made my way back to the surface.

Over dinner that night we were looking out at the sea and the moonlight sparkling on the ripples in the bay and we talked about what we had seen. 'It wasn't a very sentimental sight, was it!' said Penny and it wasn't a question. I knew exactly what she meant. It hadn't been a sight for sentiment – but then when you see the kill-or-be-killed system working before your very eyes I don't suppose it ever can be. It was a lesson. Big fish can be beautiful and often are, but lots of them only get that way by eating something else that's too small or too careless to survive.

Though Francisco arranged the papers for me each year for the *Penelope* – and looked after her all the time we were away; a debt I have yet to repay – the fact is that due to the normal delays on paperwork, I very rarely had the papers in the boat with me.

Usually this was of little importance, because the Spanish authorities often turn a blind eye to minor irregularities where tourists are concerned. And the papers for the boat were always with the Marine Commandant concerned.

But there always comes a time – it happens in any country in the world whether it comes in the shape of ticket collector or senior Civil Servant – when you meet a man who goes by the book and is not intelligent enough to use his own discretion.

My turn to meet a bureaucratic fool came when with Penny and Joanna on board I was heading out to sea from Aiguablava Bay. A big speedboat decorated with Spanish words something like 'Coast Patrol' swung in front of me and sounded repeated blasts on a car-type hooter. Penny and I waved as we would to anyone who was not actually threatening our sea lives and thump-thumped carefully around the boat and on out to sea.

My vague feeling that this seemed an over-enthusiastic welcome from a strange boat was enhanced by the fact that under a gold-braided hat sat a sailor fully rigged in orange-red life-jacket.

It all looked a bit too much like H.M.S. *Pinafore* for it was hardly life-jacket weather, but we motored on. This, obviously, was not what we were meant to do, for shouts and hooters followed our avoiding move. And there back again in front was the speedboat. And our fool.

I stopped – and knew with sinking heart that this was trouble. Any man who wore a fully inflated life-jacket in such calm sunny conditions could be nothing else. To be fair I expect that naval regulations said that life-jackets would be worn and a fool like the fool I saw before me would be a stickler for such regulations.

'Dondé es las papelas?' he shrieked.

'En San Feliu,' I shouted back. It was true. That's where the boat papers were.

His reaction was to order me to follow him to the beach. By the time I reached the place – his engine power was very superior to mine – he was all poised on the jetty, a crowd around him, ready for the show trial to begin.

The fact that it turned into a farce was hardly my fault. My Spanish is enough to cope with straightforward enquiries, but the trick of speaking any foreign language is to turn the question and answer into channels that use words you know.

My suggestion that we continue the conversation in French met with nothing, but a renewed demand for the boat's papers. This gave a wit in the crowd the chance to suggest that not only could he not speak French, but that ordinary Spanish was quite beyond him.

And this, of course, hardly helped my case. Within seconds his face was as red as his life-jacket and apoplexy seemed well within range.

Then he thought he had me. Pointing to the diving gear in the boat, he said that I had a 'fusil' there together with the diving bottles. This, of course, would have been, quite rightly, a punishable offence. No one in his right mind would carry a gun with diving bottles.

I explained carefully that it was forbidden to use such a thing with aqualung gear and showed him that what he thought was a 'fusil' was in fact a camera. The crowd, whom he had thought would be completely on his side at this humiliation of a tourist, fell about laughing. I have had many such reactions at my Spanish, but this one overwhelmed me. And brought me nearer to instant arrest.

Where were the papers for the diving bottles? These, I explained very slowly, were with the Marine Commandant at Palamos. And they were.

It seemed quite clear from his remarks that he had not the slightest idea who the Marine Commandant at Palamos was, nor in his fury did he care. I was ordered to take the boat away and tie it up, and never use it again.

This, as it was difficult to tell which was his life-jacket and which was his face, I did. It all took a little time to sort out afterwards, but we were able to use *Penelope* for the rest of the holiday.

At the time, of course, it was so infuriating that it quite ruined my day, but my friends in Aiguablava made sure that we were not inconvenienced overmuch. It does, however, give me the opportunity to say that when in Spain, do as the Spanish do, and make sure that you have papers for your boat. And if diving make sure that you have permission from the local Marine Commandant to dive. In most cases you will not encounter any difficulties – unless you meet my fool on the high seas!

However, the fool did me one service. He gave me an excuse to look again at the Lloyd's policy that I have always taken out on *Penelope*. These ship policies are an absolute joy to read.

The parts I like best contain sentences like : 'Upon any kind of goods and merchandises, and also upon the body, tackle, apparel, ordnance, munition, artillery, boat, and other furniture, of and in the good ship or vessel called the *Penelope* whereof is master under God, for this present voyage . . .'

And this : 'Touching the adventures and perils which we the assurers are contented to bear and do take upon us in this voyage : they are of the seas, men of war, fire, enemies, pirates, rovers, thieves, jettisons, letters of mart and countermart, surprisals, takings at sea, arrests, restraints, and detainments of all kings, princes and people, of what nation, condition, or quality soever, barratry of the master and mariners, and of all other perils, losses, and misfortunes, that have or shall come to the hurt, detriment, or damage of the said goods and merchandises, and ship, &c., or any part thereof.'

What category arrest by a Spanish coastal patrol comes under I am not quite sure, but a Lloyd's underwriter told me that I would not be covered by the terms of the policy. I had forgotten to read the small print attached!

The difficulty with the Costa Brava as far as boating is concerned is not risk of arrest, but the fact that it is a far windier place than many people believe. I know that I have a bit of a thing about the winds that blow at sea – mainly because the boating enthusiast has all his pleasure conditioned by them.

Whereas the yachtsman must have some wind to get his share of pleasure, that same wind has only got to increase a small amount to ruin the diver's enjoyment. Strong winds on the Sussex coast will stir up the sea and ruin visibility and though the same strength wind will not do the same to Mediterranean waters, it will make boating conditions uncomfortable.

Luck plays a large part in any diving trip and a man who is lucky with the wind is the man to have along on any such holiday abroad. Of course on the Costa Brava the winds that kick up the sea will not ruin a holiday entirely for the diver. He will usually be able to find some sheltered water somewhere – and the sun will go on shining hotly from an almost cloudless sky. That lovely sunshine is the reason that a non-boater cannot understand the discontent of a man with a boat who cannot get outside some sheltered bay. The non-boater has all he wants. Sun, sand, wine and food and all unaffected by the winds that blow in summer around the rugged headlands of the Costa Brava. It is all a matter of luck. We have stayed at Aiguablava for three weeks when each day has been perfect, the sea flat as a lake and the sun almost too hot. Or other occasions we have had our diving outside the bay curtailed by regular bouts of wind.

On the calm days we would not really make up our minds whether to turn north or south until we reached the centre of the bay. If south our target would usually be Lobster Rock. If north we would run up under the great orange rock faces of Cap Bagur, make a sharp turn under the actual point and then thump-thump would go *Penelope*'s engine until we reached Sa Tuna. There within sight of the towering white face of the 'millionaire hotel' of Cap Sa Sal we had found another rock that was a diver's paradise.

This one too broke the surface on all but the roughest days and had a similar layout to that of Lobster Rock, except that the sea around was deeper and the scenery more rugged. Here in caves on the Southern side live quite good size groupers, well-tucked in out of the spearfishermen's reach. Perhaps they have learned at last the lesson that the grouper needed to learn – not to sit at the entrance of its lair with its head out just asking to be speared – for all you will see at first as you peer into these gloomy caverns is a big dark shape well back. Any disturbance and the fish are gone deep into some inner fastness.

On the northern side the rock slopes more gradually until, split by great ravines it plunges down to over 100 feet. The life is different to that of Lobster Rock. Over these slopes hang great clouds of the chromis sea flies and the jagged surface of the slopes provides homes for octopuses, scorpion fish, and almost every kind of wrasse that is listed in the Mediterranean reference books.

But the real glory of this diving site are the great 'bushes' of green gorgonia with bright yellow tips that start at about 60 feet on the seaward end and cover all one wall with their plumage. A flash bulb fired near these 'bushes' sets the whole wall on fire with reds of every hue. And a broken off branch taken up to the surface bursts into glorious Technicolor as it comes into full sunlight. From being green with yellow tips, it is now bright red with yellow ends.

As you sit in the diving boat and look at a freshly-surfaced piece it is a shame to know that within a short while in the scorching sun, the tiny creatures that make up the colony that provides the colour will soon die and all you will be left with is a blackened, strongly-smelling twig in place of the glowing fan of only a hour before. You even have to be quick with a camera loaded with colour film to preserve the glory that was there.

I don't think I like the 'Place of the Gorgonias' as much as Lobster Rock. One gets a feeling about diving places and,

despite its beauty, I personally find this site slightly disturbing
I don't know why this is. Perhaps the deep water all around
frightens me still. Perhaps the sight of a shark's fin on the
surface before one dive alarms me even now. But the feeling is
there. And even the locals' stories of the Germans who came
there once and raised some complete amphorae does not spark
off the thrill of the possibility of finding some ancient wreck.

That, of course, is not to say that I don't keep my eyes open
for such a thing. It is the sort of place that you can make
such a discovery. In the middle of the little bay of Sa Tuna
not so far away some years ago a trainee diver made his first
descent and landed right on top of one single, perfect Phoenecian
wine jar. His discovery, of course, drove his instructors mad
with envy, but a thorough search revealed only that one. Perhaps it was a sacrifice by some ancient trader to the Gods in
exchange for fair winds and calm seas – for sacrifices of this
kind were certainly made. I hope the ancient mariner got his
wish, those cliffs around have very jagged teeth.

So we have dived and dived around Aiguablava and *Penelope*
has carried us wherever we have wanted to go. The Mediterranean here provides an almost limitless choice of different sites
and Penny and I took advantage of them whenever we could.

It provided, too, the perfect conditions for taking Kevin
when he was 13 on his first trip underwater with the aqualung
looking grotesquely huge on his back. In shallow water the conditions were the same as in a swimming pool except that there
were things for him to see that no baths manager would allow
for a moment in his pool!

The British Sub-Aqua Club lays down that its junior members
do not use compressed air breathing apparatus as a Club exercise until they are 15, when the Club feels they are adult enough
to cope with any emergency that might arise. This, I think,
is an excellent rule. But outside the Club each diving parent
must make up his mind when they think that their own particular son or daughter is ready. Kevin had been snorkelling
for many years and desperately wanted to use the aqualung.
In very shallow water I personally saw no reason to stop him
– under the strictest supervision and with constant reminders
of the basic rules. It was also an opportunity to put him through
some of the basic training so that I hope it will always be

second-nature to him. Joanna has already tried out breathing the remains of our bottles while floating on or just under the surface. Soon she will be ready too.

But very shallow water Mediterranean diving is a special kind and no one would be foolish enough, I hope, to start their children too early in the murkier waters around British coasts. Such an experience especially if conditions were really poor would certainly put a youngster off for life. This is not to denigrate diving in British waters – in many ways I prefer it to Mediterranean diving.

It is a good old-standby for an argument among divers for someone to claim either Mediterranean or British waters as the best in the world. Each side will discuss the various merits of their favourite and run down the other. 'The Mediterranean is barren compared with British waters,' says one. And to some extent and in some places he is right – but the same argument could be put forward about some bleak spots on the British diving map. 'You can never see any distance in British waters,' counters the Mediterranean champion. Well, sometimes he's right you can't, but when you can . . .

By the way, though visibility is rarely poor in the Mediterranean by normal standards, I have a theory that there the water sometimes goes cloudy *before* a storm, not the other way round. I have noticed this happen several times, but not enough to prove it is not just co-incidence. If this applies to British waters it would take a great deal of proving – there is so often a mist around!

But to go back to the British waters 'v' Mediterranean for a moment. The thing you have to realise is that each provides totally different diving, so different that it is pointless to compare them.

The Mediterranean provides you with a constant blue background and visibility of which divers dream. Even so despite this wide view it is true that in these waters – because of their great visibility – you often have to search more for the really interesting creatures. Just swimming about in wonderfully clear water must pall. The real way to enjoyment of the Med. is to look under every rock, in holes, tunnels, caves, and caverns. Then you will see that the blue sea teems with life.

British waters provide you with a green haze and, with the

exception of western and far northern waters, limited visibility. In these waters your likelihood of bumping into some piece of sea life are greatly increased. The fish often don't see you coming until you are there – and a diver, even a noisy diver, is usually a bit of a rarity to the fish so they tend to hang about that little bit longer before taking to flight.

I must confess from the photographic point of view, despite the restrictions imposed by the visibility, I prefer the unpredictability of life under the sea around our coasts. Low visibility diving doesn't worry me. But then perhaps I suffer from agrophobia (a fear of open spaces) as well as the claustrophobia that was diagnosed for me in earlier chapters of this book !

Chapter
Fifteen

I 'discovered' freshwater diving rather late in my underwater life. I suppose that sounds rather odd as one of my first trips underwater was in that freshwater lake Laughing Water, but then we were all aching to get into the big time that we believed the sea to be.

Freshwater diving isn't all that different from sea dives. It tastes different of course – a sort of soft soapy taste compared with the after shave tang of the sea. And you have to alter the amount of weight you use on your weightbelt as seawater is much more buoyant than fresh. But freshwater contains fish and weed and even mussels, though you would know immediately that you were not in the sea if you suddenly found yourself under freshwater because of the differences in the kinds of growths and creatures there.

It was Colin Doeg, the holder at that time of the title of British Underwater Photographer of the Year, who offered me the chance of taking pictures of some pike in Newbold Lake, Coventry. Not that he had the regular right to dive there. He had been invited to dive in the lake by Allan Chambers of Coventry Branch, who hold diving permission for the lake. The lake contains some monster pike, perch and carp.

When we had been suitably regaled with stories of the huge fish which other divers had seen we slipped into wet suits despite the blazing hot June sun and carried the gear down to the water's edge.

My confidence was not helped by the small boy who shouted to me just as I was about to submerge: 'Watch out for the monster pike, mister!' Allan led the way and Colin and I followed him. Once below about 25 feet the reason for the wet suits became paralysingly obvious. The lake had a proper thermocline in it – a thermocline roughly speaking being a line where waters of two different temperatures meet. At 80 feet on the bottom it seemed freezing. Visibility was, the Coventry divers assured me later, very poor for the lake. I made it about 10 feet. And at depth there was no sign of a fish.

Pike, I had read only the night before while doing some research, liked to be in among reeds to feed on the unsuspecting small fish that passed by. So I headed up for the reeds that grew around the banks. Closer to the surface the visibility was better and there seemed plenty of small fry in the water. I cruised along below the root level of the reeds looking up at the surface. Green 'aquarium' weed carpeted the bank up which I was looking and some tall water plants lifted their way towards the surface. It was all rather pretty.

My first sight of a pike came just at that moment, but for a moment I almost refused to believe what my eyes were telling me. I thought it was a piece of driftwood of which there was quite a bit about. A big still dark shape was the pike. And only the constant fanning of his fins gave him away. He was in a gap in the weeds where small debris had collected against the silvery surface.

I found this technique of looking up towards the surface was the best way of spotting the fish. For no sooner had I seen one and lifted my camera sight to my eye while finning stealthily up and forward, than I saw another.

Both fishes bore the same markings – a mottled dark brown with darker speckling and barring. The larger one seemed to be paler than the other.

But the thing that really impressed me about pike was the fact that they appeared not to be the slightest bit frightened of the diver. They would hang still, almost curious, at your approach apparently studying you with big cold eyes. When you got within touching distance they would glide slowly away. Many fish do not like turning their back on you when moving slowly like this, but not the pike. He would present his big powerful tail to you contemptuously, though you got the feeling you were still being watched over his shoulder.

This slow withdrawal by the fish from the scene obviously presented great difficulties if you were trying to take pictures of the fish as I was. Quite by accident I found a method of dealing with it.

If you swam outside the fish – between him and the open

water outside the reeds – he would turn into the reeds and when a foot inside cover hang motionless once again. The barring on the pike's sides provided very good camouflage once he had done this. So good that if you took your eyes off one for a second, you were unlikely to spot him again. The pike, too, seemed able to slide through close-together reed stems without disturbing them in the slightest. Perhaps they did in fact touch the stems, but it didn't look like it.

Once you had your pike in this position in the reeds it was often possible to part the weeds and manoeuvre the camera gently into position. Any swift movement of the camera at this stage would give you a one-second display of the power and speed of the pike and he would be gone.

While parting the reeds to do this on one occasion I gave myself a real fright. As I pushed the stems gently out of the way I came face to face with another pike that had chosen the same hiding place as the one I was trying to photograph. My fingers – bare fingers – must have brushed his nose. For a moment we stared at each other – so close that I found difficulty in focusing my eyes on that lethal nose – and then he slid away.

Only twice on that dive did I see a pike take aggressive action – if it could be interpreted as that. The first happened when I was photographing a real baby – it was all of 12 inches long. This little one was letting me pull weed out of the way all around him and even lift a dead tree branch he was hiding under out of the way of the camera. I was just about to take a second picture when something made me look over my shoulder. I was just in time to see a whitish monster fully three feet long heading quietly but purposefully towards me. Of course it may not have been an aggressive action, but my violent reaction – I span round in the water – sent him away very fast.

Dr John Lythgoe, who has great experience of photographing freshwater fish, particularly pike, didn't think that the pike was intending violence on me when I told him about this. He has found that pike tend to move in when the bottom is disturbed as they think that the kicked up debris may indicate a fish in trouble and a possible feed. Well, it is true that in moving the tree branch I did disturb the lake bed – in fact I was waiting for the water to clear for the second picture when I saw the big pike. So he may well be right.

The second occasion when there was some indication of aggression came when I had manoeuvred the head of the flash gun to within a few inches of another pike's nose. Suddenly he put his head down and bucked at it. I can only describe it as a bucking action – he looked for all the world like a stallion pawing at the ground before charging. But he fled when I moved the flash again. If the flash head had held a polished reflector one could have suspected that he was about to attack his own reflection, but the inside of the Nikinos flash bowl is satin-finished.

Pike are funny about flash. Flashbulbs going off right in their eyes do not seem to upset them at all. The pike hang quite still, mouth closed, but with the fins at the side of the long mouth going all the time. They behave rather like wrasse in the sea with their long unhurried swings in and out of weed. And the long nose is as prominent underwater as it is deadly to other fish.

I saw one of the pike that day strike at a school of small fry. One moment the fish was absolutely still, the next it had sprung forward, there was a gap in the ranks of the little fry, and the fish was back in position as though it had never moved at all. It was a demonstration of speed and efficiency that leaves many sea fish standing. It shows what that thickening of the pike towards the big tail is all about – the power supply of a killer.

I made one 50 cubic foot bottle of air last 55 minutes on that first dive, changed bottles, used up another one and then switched to snorkel so that I could carry on looking at these magnificent fish. In all we were in the water from 11.30 in the morning until four in the afternoon with a short break for a rest and a sandwich lunch. That's one thing to be said for lake diving, you don't have to worry about the tides!

Colin Doeg spent the same time in the water. Going down the M.1. we both had a go at driving the car. We were physically tired, but so interested in what we had seen that we didn't stop talking the whole way.

We agreed that the main point about pike is that they look sinister – mainly because nothing about a diver really seems to disturb them – not aqualung bubbles, nor panting through a snorkel tube, nor the bright orange and yellows of our lifejackets. The only thing that did seem to put them off is a really violent movement, but even this didn't seem to disturb them for very long.

They give the impression that they know that nothing in that lake will hurt them – that they are the kings of all that they survey. During the dive I had seen about a dozen big pike and some tiddlers. Anglers fish the lake regularly and the pike give them good sport, but not I'll bet half the pleasure and excitement that they had given me that afternoon.

Not all dives, of course, work out to plan. Not all, of course, are beautiful. Fresh in my memory is an experiment that failed. Having done a great deal of diving on the north side of the Mixon Hole (it really is a great hole in the seabed) – that is the side nearest to Selsey Bill itself – we decided that the south side would repay a visit. We imagined that this unexplored territory off the coast of Sussex – unexplored that is as far as we were concerned – would imitate the steep ravines of the opposite face.

The Mixon Hole is in fact rather like an elongated dustpan. The north side is the side nearest the handle and the fall from 30 feet at low tide to the seabed is steep, although there are one or two shelves on the way down to the bottom at 75 feet.

A quick echo-sounder trip across the Hole had led us to believe that the south side was similar. In fact we had taken the echo-sounder traverse much too quickly and what showed up as a steep cliff was in fact a more gentle slope down to the bottom of the pan. So just as a dustpan tends to curve upward to its lip so the Mixon hole on the south side was much more gentle than we imagined.

John and Geoff Bowden had explored this south face on one previous dive and thought they had missed the steep sides by some distance. All they had found was a bed of shingle and shells that extended gently – with some banks on the way – down to the floor of the Mixon.

So we decided on a double experiment. As the tides were generally not suitable on this particular week-end – you have to reach the Mixon some two hours before low tide to be sure of slack water – we decided to see if the same sort of slack existed close to high water. A long time ago some divers had told me that if you set off to cross the Mixon Hole underwater you would never make it as the tide swept through at a rate of knots. And we knew that the tide there can be particularly fierce from our own experience. Previously we had to pick up divers some distance away when the tide on the surface swept them away, though down below there would be little or no tidal movement.

So we decided to find out about tides at or near high water and at the same time find out whether there was a steep south side to the Mixon Hole. We found out both, though I hardly think that made the experiment a success.

After anchoring on the south side with the echo-sounder showing a depth of 40 feet, Penny and I entered the water.

That is not to say that we both went in together. I went first and arranged to meet her at the bottom of the anchor rope. As soon as I had surfaced after toppling backwards into the water I knew that this was going to be one of those dives.

Only by flat-out finning could I beat the surface current and reach the anchor rope at the bow of the boat. But this was no reason to call the dive off at once. It sometimes happens that this surface tidal stream falls off dramatically the deeper you go down and so I hauled myself steadily down the bar-tight anchor rope. As I went down hand over hand I hoped that soon I would turn back from being a piece of washing fluttering in the current out from the anchor rope into a civilised diver in the still of the deep.

It was not to be. Visibility on the way down was perhaps 15 feet. Ahead of me the hemp of the rope stretched out like a brown arrow pointing down at a very shallow angle. I remember thinking that they certainly had plenty of rope out. The water was visible streaming past. That is to say that the suspended sediment in the water was making the trip down the anchor rope seem as though I was pushing forward into a granulated green fog. Every now and then a recognisable piece of torn-off weed would loom into view at the limit of visibility, move slowly towards you, green and brown, and then hurtle past on the wings of the tide.

I was now feeling distinctly unhappy about the possibilities of this dive. The bottom came into view. A grey bottom. Then closer, a bottom made up of hundreds of thousands of slipper limpet shells with here and there a painted top-shell just to break up the mounds of slippers.

The tide was just as strong and when I dug my heels into the shells to ease the pull on my arms a grey cloud of sediment arose for a short distance from the sea bed and was then whirled away out of sight.

This was to be drift dive and we were certainly going to drift! I could feel the jerking of the anchor rope telling me that Penny was on her way down to join me. As soon as she arrived we sorted ourslves out, linked hands firmly and let go. The rate of travel over the bottom was amazing. Single brown fronds of laminaria that had found enough grip for the hold-fast on a large stone lay flat along the shingle and shells. We swept over them like a V-bomber on an approach run.

The camera round my neck was useless – but it wouldn't have been if I could have stopped to take a picture. Visibility was not too bad – 10–15 feet.

My free hand was still clutching my camera when I realised that we were right over a real photograph. Hugging the shingle was a 3-foot wide black diamond. From one of the shallow angles of it a tail stretched out another foot. And two eyes watched us anxiously and the creature flinched as we whizzed over it. I dug my heels in and attempted to turn at the same time bringing the camera up. A shower of shells and other debris cascaded over the thornback ray and this disturbance was too much for it.

For a moment as it rose from its resting place the tide whirled it along with us, and Penny's hand tightened convulsively on mine. She had only just seen it. Then the ray headed down the gentle slope into deeper water. For a while we tried to follow it but at 60 feet it turned into the tide and with curling beats of its 'wings' was able to work across the tide on a route that no matter how hard we tried we could not follow. For another ten minutes we drifted at speed across the same featureless slope before I decided that we were unlikely to see anything more.

I twisted the control knob on the Fenzy life-jacket and a shrill squeak heralded the air pouring into the buoyancy chamber. We lifted up and gently, still travelling with the tide, made our way towards the surface.

Even this, for me, was not without its unpleasant side. I had wasted half a bottle of air, and had no pictures to show for my dive. On the credit side we had seen a big thornback, but even this was outweighed by the pain I suddenly felt in my right ear. Something I had always hoped would not happen seemed to be about to. I eased the ascent still more by releasing air from my life-jacket. The pain grew worse. My right ear would not clear.

All the stories I had read about this unpleasant phenomenon seemed about to become true. A famous French diver had this trouble and finally running out of air had to push up to the surface without any choice. His ear – really the Eustachian tube to the inner ear – was blocked and as the expanding air had to come out somewhere it, so the story ran, finally pushed his eye out in its attempts to escape. I knew in the moment I got the pain that I was in similiar trouble. But, thank heavens it wasn't so serious. There was a series of explosions inside my ear and we hit the surface at the same moment. I felt sick and my ear was making appalling squeaking noises, but my eardrum felt intact. And the boat which had been following our marker buoy was right beside us.

Once back in the boat copious applications of 'Cleer' – anti-congestant you could buy at chemists in a small blue plastic squeeze-bottle – finally got through and my ear popped back to normal. But a stuffed up slightly deaf feeling persisted for several days.

This ear trouble surprised me. For the previous three weeks on holiday in Spain I had been diving every day without the slightest trouble. I had no trouble either clearing my ears on the descent to the Mixon Hole. Yet on the ascent ... There seemed no logical explanation. I suppose that now I shall add fear of ascents to all my other fears!

Our discontent with this dive was multiplied when John and Geoff went down only minutes later on the north side under the sheer wall of clay and experienced nothing like the same tide troubles. We can only assume that the tide, due to the shape of the Hole, sets up curious swirling movements. We know however that there is little point in diving on the south side of the Mixon at or near high tide. John rated that a successful experiment!

Major Hume Wallace, the Administrative Agent of the British Sub-Aqua Club and president of the Kingston-on-Thames Branch, is conducting an archaeological and geological survey into the area around the Mixon.

He believes this to be an ancient Roman port and if you look at the chart of the area he has good reason for this belief. When you add to this the fact that he has found and raised a Roman ballista ball four feet in circumference, one of many at the foot of the cliff on the north side of the Mixon Hole, there is little room for doubt. Those ancient catapults were not things you put just anywhere along the coast.

In fact while diving down the Hole itself close to the southern edge, I saw on one drift dive, two remarkable circular rocks half-buried in the shingle. I suspect that the ancient artillerymen used up many more balls in practice – or with war-like intent – than have yet been discovered.

Until we had found the Far Mulberry, I had despaired of finding a wreck within diveable distance of Bognor. After we found that I really gave up researching for another – there seemed no further point from which I could start. No one knew of any nearby. There was a vague report of an aircraft down in the sea somewhere off the coast, but 'somewhere' can be anywhere in the vastness of the sea.

'Somewhere around here' is the phrase that makes a diver's heart sink when he is trying to help somebody find something lost overboard. Only a diver knows how easily he can miss something quite huge in low visibility waters – and how big the sea really is when you start looking for lost property underwater.

People who assure you that they know exactly where it is lose their shore confidence when faced at sea with identifying the exact spot.

So it is with wrecks. In many cases wrecks have been found by accident. In others, of course, the position of the wreck is found by long research among dirty dusty documents. Alexander McKee, amateur diver and naval historian, looked for the site of Henry VIII's man o'war, the *Mary Rose,* for years before finding her position marked on an old chart of the Portsmouth coast. And then dived to confirm it.

Further east a group of divers from the Brighton Branch of the British Sub-Aqua Club found by chance a four-engined bomber underwater – a relic of some wartime battle – when diving to free a fisherman's caught-up nets.

Down in the West Country, Bernard Rogers and Roy Davis found the wreck of the *Mohegan* by doing their research first and then diving where it ought to be, and further west still, a lone snorkeller out for some fun discovered what may prove to be the earliest shipwreck yet found around the coasts of Britain.

And so it goes – pure chance may put you on to some unknown wreck. And this is all part of the thrill of diving. Penny and I made a minor discovery on one of those 'somewhere around here' dives near Bognor. We were searching for a string of lobster pots lost by two local fishermen. Their marks were good, but as all their markers had been torn away in the previous week's gales it was definitely a somewhere-around-here dive on Bognor Ledge.

Visibility was poor – between 3 and 5 feet – and as we circled the area I knew that we had little chance of finding the pots. The gales had been heavy and the pots could have been moved by the big seas. The water was still full of suspended particles of sand and other debris.

This sand and muck will settle provided the sea remains calm for a week or two and then every frond of laminaria will be powdered with it so that when you shake or even just touch the weed the debris will float down back to the seabed.

Penny looked at me from her position at my side and extended her arms in a shrug of hopelessness. I nodded agreement, but we went on looking. On the Ledge itself the sea had been hard at work. Most of the laminaria had lost its foliage and only the shattered torn stumps remained. It was rather like flying over a forest that had been heavily shelled by artillery.

And it was because the foliage had been ripped away that, almost as my air was coming to an end, I saw something down on the rocks. Man made wreckage is usually totally different in shape to that of nature-fashioned rocks. This was a great long slab of something. It was too much of a straight line with parallel sides to be natural. At first I thought it was a cannon.

Penny prodded at it with her diving knife and the give-away black cloud of decomposing iron rose in the water. Then I saw that no cannon could be like this, it had no mouth for a start. Was it some great anchor stock? We chipped away at the concretion that held it down to the seabed at each end without much success.

My air was running out, but I motioned to Penny to stay with the object and made a complete circular sweep around her, just keeping her dim shape in vision through the murky water. I hoped to find more wreckage, but what I found was unexpected. Another man shaped object caught my eye. I jerked it out from under a rock.

In my hands I held a thin – one-inch deep – paving stone. Badly worn and about a foot square with one corner broken off, it was still definitely a paving stone. There was nothing else nearby.

I returned to Penny who was still working to free the object. I pulled at it and it broke to pieces. From the middle of a six-inch cast of concretions some metal fell into my hands. It was a strip of iron about four inches deep with a perfect hole drilled or cast through the centre. The decomposing iron had all fallen away and the surface looked almost bright. But it was only part of a great long bar. My air was finished and bringing only the small salvaged piece with me I had to surface.

For a moment underwater I thought we had made a great discovery. But it seems we hadn't. Certainly from the amount of growth and concretion on my slab of metal it may have been there for at least a century. But why the paving stone? Did some ship get smashed on to the Ledge by a storm to-gether with a cargo of one paving stone? Or was it just a small boat with a paving stone to use as a fishing weight? Who knows? Who will ever know? It's just another piece of wreckage 'some-where out there'.

Chapter
Sixteen

It is 59 and one-tenth miles exactly from my house to Bognor Regis Yacht Club – a car journey that when conditions are right takes about an hour and a half. To get those conditions right at week-ends in the height of the summer means getting up and off very early.

If you leave it just half-an-hour late on a morning when the sun shines, you can abandon all hope of doing the journey quickly and must then plunge into the twisting back roads to avoid coming to a complete halt in some steaming traffic jam. The same 'back way' is the only way home on a Sunday evening, though you cannot of course avoid complete contact with the main roads.

Despite these difficulties, most week-ends we would say that the diving is worth much more than any hold-ups on the way home. And the landlord of the little pub called 'The Plough' at which we stop for a break when well over half-way home must think us very strange customers indeed. The talk is all of fish and lobsters, running out of air, winds and waves, weed and rocks, vis and poor vis, bottles and weights, and so on until it's time to get on the road again. So we say 'Good night,' and from the wrinkled condition of the landlord's brow, he still can't make out what all our chatter is about.

He must have been even more puzzled about our enthusiasm after what turned out to be almost the last dive of last season. Because on that Sunday we had found a new diving site. It would have to have been almost the last dive of the year, but that's how things happen. Our new site was found not entirely by luck – though of course that played a part – because the Ferrograph tracer echo-sounder brought us right on to it. Mist had clamped down blotting out most of the shore, but by one or two marks still remaining we got into a position that we thought might be worth investigating.

Geoff Bowden dived first. John and I kitted up and while we did so kept the boat following the marker buoy with its orange rope down to the diver far below. Well, it wasn't all that far because the echo-sounder showed the tip of a shelf of some kind in 45 feet of water. But what was interesting was the steep fall away to much deeper water.

When Geoff surfaced he was enthusiastic about all the life – and lobsters – that he'd seen. And John and I were in the water almost as soon as he was back in the boat. And we dived into something super.

We found ourselves on a hump of low rocks and short weed. The top was like a plateau, level and broken only by small clumps of rocks. Between these clumps were shingle, sand and shells. Visibility was a good 20 feet and the water shimmered over the top of the hump.

I have seen this sort of dancing haze effect before, but only in the Mediterranean. I am not quite sure what causes it, but suspect that it is light reflecting from the sides of the shingle stones and then being broken up again by the darkness of the rocks. The weed being short gave a sort of purple sheen to the whole outlook. But this was not the cause of our pleasure. It was the life that we found there.

Fish darted in all directions. Wrasse and blennies squiggled about low down on the seabed. This movement of fish added to the shimmer of the sea. More was to come. As we moved over this hump in the sea, one side dropped away fairly steeply to a uniform seabed of sand, mud and more slipper limpet shells. This wall was the most amazing sight of all. Lobsters, big lobsters, sat in the open outside their holes under the low rocks that projected from the steep slope. Their red antennae stood out as did the almost-yellow outlines of their claws, and their bodies were a blue so deep that it was almost black.

At our approach one – with left-hand claw missing and only the big crusher remaining – shot down and away propelling himself along backwards with great flips of his powerful tail. The others crouched and took up defensive positions with claws uplifted ready for a fight.

We wouldn't have been human if we hadn't looked at this hillside of lobsters with amazement and then greed. So we took the biggest ones – one gave me a nasty nip in the struggle to get a hand over the claws and round the back – but left this undersea larder well stocked. For it wasn't just a meeting place for big lobsters – some looked over two feet long, but weighed in at about three pounds – there were many more little ones to be seen in smaller holes.

Soon, too soon, our air was gone and it was Geoff's turn again. I decided to join him, but it was some time before I had changed over demand valve and harness to a new bottle and was diving down the line of the marker buoy to join him on the seabed. I knew within seconds of starting down that conditions had changed. The tide had started to run hard and it took a long time to get to the bottom. Gone was the shimmering light and down by Geoff's side the water was green and gloomy.

There was no question now of fighting the tide and when Geoff ran low on air and handed over the marker buoy arm loop to me, it started to tighten hard around my biceps. In fact, though at first I thought it was Geoff making his way up the line to the boat, the drag of the buoy became quite painful even through the cushion of the neoprene wet suit material.

The tide slid me over the bottom. I had lost the hump in the sea – indeed I doubt if I could have stayed on it in that tide despite the rocks that were there to cling to. The seabed was shingle now and a glance at my depth gauge told me that I was travelling slowly downwards at a depth of about 80 feet.

A big dogfish, the lesser spotted kind, lay on the bottom still, as though asleep, head to tide. I tapped him gently on the head as I glided over him and even this only made him shift position just a little. The visibility was worse, but this must have been due to the depth and the bottle green of the water. I looked at my pressure gauge and, as though in a dream, noted that the needle was so far in the red that I must go up. But a sort of doziness was upon me and, for some reason or non-reason, I ignored it and let the tide carry me on over the bottom. And all the time a little nagging in the back of my brain told me to go up.

I felt no fear – which is strange for me – and was vaguely puzzled at the shortage of air. Surely I had only been down about 3 minutes? (In fact it was at least 15) And only when breathing became completely tight did I head up towards the surface. When I was still only just coming into the full glow of light from the surface I was completely out of air. My bottle gave me one last half-drag and at the same moment I broke out into the light. Even then I felt very surprised that I had used so much air in such a short time.

Plain stupidity. That is my verdict now on my reactions during that dive. It was obvious at that depth I would be using air in great gouts, but the lesson learned is that a gently sloping shingle seabed – at the time the slope could not have been all that gentle – is one to watch with great care. Following such an undistinguished bottom with no sharp features to give you a reference point can lead you into very deep water indeed.

Still, we have found a new site. A new place to dive where the life is different once again. Different from the Mixon Hole with its ravines and sheer cliff walls, different from the Far Mulberry with its schools of pollack and pouting. Different in fact from anything we have seen in our area of Sussex seabed. And next year we know we'll find something different somewhere else.

So, as I write this last chapter, another diving season is coming to an end. The gales of autumn are becoming more and more frequent and the wind out in the diving boat on the last of our dives evaporated the water off the outside of our wet suits and made us shiver despite the watery sun.

But though my diving season is coming to an end other divers admit no season and push on through the winter and out into spring again. That was all right when the first enthusiasms for diving burned so bright that no icy water could damp them down, but not now.

Not that I would like you to think that I am singing 'September Song' over my diving life. If 'the days dwindle down to a precious few' it is because of the approach of this winter not the frost of old age.

I am not considering giving up diving, but just at the stage where I wonder on some days whether it is worth going in at all when it is obviously going to be very uncomfortable. Colin Doeg and I were talking the other day about refusing to give up diving at all. We visualised being pushed down to the water in wheel-chairs and being tipped into the water. The problem of recovering the old gentlemen has still to be solved, but we're working on it!

How long in fact can you go on diving? Surgeon Rear-Admiral Stanley Miles, who until recently was in charge of the medical aspects of all the Royal Navy's diving, and is the author of the standard medical work on the subject called *Underwater Medicine* is the man who should know. In an article, reproduced here by kind permission of Bernard Eaton the Editor of the British Sub-Aqua Club's magazine, *Triton*, he wrote:

'At what age should a man (or woman) stop diving? This question is repeatedly asked, but of course there is no real answer other than to say that age as such has nothing to do with the ability to dive.

Age when expressed as a number of years, is no more than a measure of the time that has passed since birth. There are those who die of old age in their fifties and others who reach a hundred. There are many in their forties who are quite unfit to dive and others still diving in their eighties.

It is, of course, very tempting to put an upper age limit on all kinds of specific activities – not only diving – but this is sheer laziness. It does no more than relieve the doctor of the responsibility of examining the so-called 'over-age' man to determine whether he is or is not physically and mentally fit.

Diving is an occupation to which those of maturer years are often more completely adapted. With the normal process of ageing, there is a mellowing of temperament and a progressive increase in ability to economise in muscular effort, two features which are desirable in all underwater activity. Experience is thus a major factor from which the ageing diver quite naturally learns to appreciate his limitations. He is much less likely to run into trouble from over doing it than the younger over-enthusiastic beginner.

Age is therefore no barrier to diving. It does, however, demand some additional consideration for it is in the older age groups that such conditions, unacceptable to diving, as respiratory illness, high blood pressure and potential heart disease are more common.

When an older man or woman is being considered for diving, it is the full medical examination which must be the final deciding factor. This must be thorough and should include, in addition to conventional investigations, a chest X-ray, repeated blood pressure readings, an exercise tolerance test, and, if possible, an electrocardiograph. Just as it is impossible to give an upper age limit, so it is undesirable to put a firm limit on blood pressure. This, too, must be considered in relation to the examination as a whole.

The mental attitude of the diver is also important. If he is to continue, there must be the general desire and confidence to do so. Frequently a diver of many years' experience will, in his advancing years, ask the doctor whether or not at his age he should continue. This may be the result of a sub-conscious feeling that the time has come to give up diving, but pride may be saying continue. In such cases, a doctor's advice, following a thorough examination, to give up would be very proper and, indeed, received with relief.

The decision must therefore not be taken on age alone. Diving, may, if of a gentle and supervised nature, even be of benefit to the aged.'

However, by the time the wheelchair calls for me, I'm sure that the whole of diving in Britain will have changed. The phenomenal growth of the British Sub-Aqua Club, the governing body for the sport of underwater swimming in this country, shows no sign of slackening. And though now the sight of a boat-load of divers is no uncommon sight, then it will be common – so common that it will excite no interest apart from the casual glance. The silly row between divers and fishermen about shellfish will have been settled long ago and divers will act as spotters for the fishermen reporting to them new places worth fishing.

I hope that then too the work done by the amateur divers of Britain will be fully recognised. As I write this there are men and women giving up all their spare time to underwater archaeology, tracing and bringing to light new facts about the history of the seaborne traffic to and from this island of ours.

Other divers are taking geology underwater, helping to track down our even earlier past by the stories that seabed outcrops of rocks have to tell. And more and more 'week-end divers' are turning to underwater photography to record the life and behaviour of marine creatures as they are and not unnaturally cooped up in some marine aquarium.

Divers are studying sea levels, now and in ancient times, the effect that the sea has on our weather, how weeds affect our shoreline, testing new equipment, taking part in fact in a giant investigation of the sea which gathers speed and momentum as more and more new divers are trained to use underwater equipment. This is probably the greatest single contribution being made to the future by the British Sub-Aqua Club. Their system of training is copied all over the world and in Britain and overseas the Club is steadily training more and more divers.

Already there are enough amateur divers in Britain to provide, when grouped together, proper and scientific investigations of one of today's greatest problems – the growth of pollution.

Already Britain's divers have twice given up a great deal of their spare time to combine in a massive research study into the effects of pollution on the life cycle of the creatures under the sea. This work has involved the properly recorded collection of weeds, sea urchins and starfish from sites all round the British Isles.

These divers are helping to make sure that our children's children do not suddenly wake up to find their children have grown up not knowing what a 'free-range' fish tastes like – and that man has sterilised the sea.

A remote risk? Not so. Day by day we pump the muck of our world into the sea, so that pollution creeps unseen – except by divers – beneath the oceans of the world. So that already dozens of species are extinct. So that a normally harmless creature like the Crown of Thorns starfish suddenly suffers a population explosion and eats to death the reefs protecting the dream islands of coral seas. So that all of a sudden the sea may become a menace, not a source of food and wonder.

Any diver will tell you that not all the danger comes from hideous things like sewage and atomic waste and poison gases, but that the products of our plastic society are beginning to be a common sight on the seabed. That the indiscriminate tipping of this sort of rubbish is on the increase. That nothing will destroy a plastic cup, or knife, or fork, or plate and that the passenger ships and ferries are dumping this material in sackfuls into the sea on each and every trip. In the past a lazy crew might throw away the dirty cutlery rather than wash it, but in saving the washing up by using plastic substitutes which do not rust and disappear, we are killing the fish.

Nothing in the sea that we yet know of will destroy this plastic – nor will the gastric juices in the stomachs of the fish which swallow it as it flutters like temptation down to them. So too, lost or abandoned fishing nets with meshes made of plastic will go on fishing for ever and each set of rotting corpses will only make way for more.

The truth is that we are all guilty of polluting the sea. The man who overfills his outboard so that petrol films out over the surrounding water . . . the managing director who decides on waste disposal into river or sea to save a copper on the balance sheet . . . they both do it. So does the man who fights against a rate increase for his seaside flat, a rate increase that was to provide for an inland sewage disposal plant. And so do the local politicians who decide, rather than risk disfavour, to go on pumping out sewage untreated into the sea.

The sea is exhaustible. We have had our warning loud and clear from the sterile fishless lakes of North America. Divers too get warnings when they notice the thinning of the shoals of fish around some favoured spot and know that though this once could be put down to seasonal fluctuations, now we can't be sure. Fishermen whose catches don't come up to standard year after year are getting the same warning. And we all do too little about it.

Man must in the end learn to live with the sea not destroy it. The same thing must come about in his relationship with the creatures of the sea.

When I described in the first chapter of this book Raymond Bethoux's meeting with a moray eel – and my first sight of one – it was a meeting that ended in the death of the moray. Yet I have since found out, as I wrote there, that there are divers who have stroked and almost tamed this 'killer'.

I am not suggesting that man will ever become friends with the sharks, but more and more divers are finding out that fish are approachable and some sort of relationship can be established with them.

The pouting of the Far Mulberry do not, I think, fear me and my fellow divers. They can be touched, though it is doubtful if this essentially human form of contact is necessary or desirable.

214

Tony Baverstock, a well-known Brighton diver, has told me of others who have stroked young conger eels and found their reactions similar to those of kittens. A John Dory which we met over the remains of the sailing ship *Andola*, which was wrecked on Shark's Fin near the Manacles in Cornwall in 1895, has allowed Penny and I to stroke it, or rather tickle it under the chin, without any sign that it found this contact violently disagreeable.

What this really means is that divers are in the position that primitive man was in on his first approach to all the creatures of the earth. Primitive man of course had his reasons for making that first approach one of violence. In the violent world of today it is comforting to know that many divers have abandoned the 'shoot-first-and-ask-questions-afterwards' technique in their dealing with the creatures they meet in man's first mass penetration into that Inner Space we call the sea.

But it seems clear that unless we all do more to stop the murder of the sea itself, there will be no point in the divers learning to live with the fish. There will be no point in the penetration of Inner Space, because there will be no fish left to live with – and the sea will be as barren as the surface of the moon has finally proved to be.

Index

219